# Bitter or Better:
# The Melisa Schonfield Story

by

The Inmate Formerly Known as 15G0717

DORRANCE
PUBLISHING CO
EST. 1920
PITTSBURGH, PENNSYLVANIA 15238

Dorrance Publishing Co
585 Alpha Drive
Pittsburgh, PA 15238
Visit our website at *www.dorrancebookstore.com*

**ISBN**: 978-1-6495-7243-1
**eISBN**: 978-1-6495-7751-1

# DEDICATION

I would like to thank my family and friends who stood by me through sick and sin. In spite of how it ended, I want to thank my ex-husband for a hell of a ride and two great children. Chapter two of my life would not be possible otherwise. My brother showed me loyalty even when I did not think I deserved it. His endless encouragement while I faced fear and despair is unmeasurable. I lost my dad Thanksgiving of 2019. My dad stood by me unconditionally. His lifelong and unconditional love guided me through the good, the bad, and the ugly. He never gave up on me.

Never underestimate the kindness and compassion of strangers when you feel you have lost everything. The women in green picked me up and gave me the strength to be better not bitter. The most socioeconomically diverse group of women became my kin, my family. We had each other's back. There were several correction officers that made incarceration tolerable. Not all COs are out to make an offender's life miserable. The ladies in green, a.k.a. Sisters of the Sorority of Misfits, helped me become the best version of myself. Remember, "sunshine and rainbows."

This book is dedicated to my daughter and her son, who made things happen when I thought my circumstances were impossible. They made me feel visible and loved. Her son is the little boy I tried to keep safe. My grandson kept my hopes and dreams alive as only a child could. I love you more than all the fish in the ocean and the stars in the sky.

And SHE lived happily ever after....

This Memoir is excerpts from my prison journal
hence some of the disorderly transitions or lack
thereof just like prison life.

# FOREWORD

When the news first broke, it shocked everyone. Melisa Schonfield, a 57-year-old wife, mother and grandmother, a therapist, was accused of hiring a hitman to murder the father of her grandson. Police claimed this well-respected and successful woman in Watertown, New York, who was married to a "prominent dentist" at the time, met an undercover detective at a local Walmart parking lot and provided a $5,500 down payment, half of the agreed-upon $11,000, to end the life of the man she said was abusing her daughter and grandson. She was pulled over minutes after leaving, arrested, and after pleading guilty to second-degree attempted murder, she would be sentenced to five years in prison. While incarcerated, separated from the daughter and grandchild she sought to protect, her health would rapidly decline. About halfway through, her husband would file for divorce. This family is the last place where you would expect to find a murder-for-hire plot. These were esteemed members of the community. Melisa was a Licensed Certified Social Worker with an R privilege—she has more than six years of supervision. She specialized in couple or marital issues, depression, interpersonal relationships, parenting issues, stress, anxiety, behavioral problems, and personality disorders. There was a hidden side of abuse few people knew about, some buried in Melisa's own childhood, and began to resurface with her own daughter, due to the relationship experience with her grandson's father. She seems like a typical mom and grandma, which she is. When you think of a person imprisoned for hiring a hitman, she is not what you would imagine. White, upper-middle-class devoted mother of two, with graying hair and youthful skin and a cane, she is a fascinating combination of humility and fury. She does not see herself as a victim, and she readily owns responsibility for the crime she attempted to commit. She has deep regrets, still struggling to reconcile the conscience of a moral life with the fact that she attempted to have someone killed. How did she wind up here? This woman, who was motivated by fear, could not see any other choices, and in a frenzy of desperation and despair, plotted and paid for a murder. A mother who saw no other way to protect her family. A wife deeply devoted to her marriage that would later betray her; a grandmother who took in her grandson only to be separated from him for five years. A woman pushed to the edge. A woman who went that far and paid the price. A woman who did what so many of us wonder if we might do—make the problem go away by any means necessary. This is the story that speaks to all of us, not only in our personal lives, however they may unfold, but also to the society we all live in that is riddled with system failures. A mental health expert who did not seek help from the institutions designed to assist her when she was suffering from a mental breakdown, law enforcement that turned its back to the persistent harassment and threats from the father, a judicial process that showcased her crime for clickbait, a prison system with no means for rehabilitation, no competency to address her desperately needed medical care. Even the aftermath of Melisa's release was fraught with system failures. This is a story of what can happen to a person when they believe the societal institutions failed them. From maternal to marital to medical to legal to the punitive failed. And ultimately, this is a story of personal triumph, how a prisoner freed herself from the prison of her mind. This is a story that could happen to anyone.

—Elizabeth Shepard

# PREFACE: JUST THE FACTS

This is my daily personal journal. In retrospect this documents the transformation from an imprisoned J-Bird to the Free Bird I am today.

One year and three months prior to my arrest, our daughter Alexis, wound up moving back in with my husband and me when her son, Eli, was three months old. The abusive situation between my daughter and the baby's father became too dangerous, so we got her out on Thanksgiving weekend, when the baby's father was away. It was very stressful in and of itself—having a grown, wounded daughter and her dogs and her baby living in our house—and while I was relieved to be in a position to help her, our daily life only got worse.

We nicknamed Eli's father "Piece of Shit Sperm Donor," or POSSD. That is all he ever was to me. POSSD continued to harass Alexis, calling and texting incessantly, threatening and stalking her from afar. He would directly and indirectly threaten Alexis. I got the idea from his threats that he was planning on taking the baby to another country and she would never see him again. It never seemed like it was going to end. It was like poking somebody over and over again. The constant provocations, the helplessness, the strain, the fear of what was going to happen to my daughter and grandson if he made good on his word—my terror became overwhelming, all-consuming, larger-than-life. I just lost it. I vowed to keep them safe by any means necessary.

Systems are in place to protect abused women and children. Few people know these systems better than I do—in fact, I have counseled people for years to solicit help from these systems. And we tried to use them. Alexis called the police several times to report his harassment and threats, asking for protection, and even a restraining order. But the calls only resulted in a slap-on-POSSD's-wrist. When confronted, he would be so polite, so agreeable. He would say, "Yes, yes, Officer, I understand. I am so sorry, you have my word, I'm not going to do this again." He lied. Alexis could have called Child Protective Services, and Alexis contemplated this for months, but it came with risks. I feared if Child Protective Services got involved, somehow or another my grandson would be separated not only from his dangerous father but also from his nurturing mother, and despite her petition for sole custody, Eli might wind up in foster care.

Alexis, my husband at the time, and I could have gone to counseling to manage the anxiety, fear, and resentment that was festering in our house like an open wound. But in the height of it all, this seemed silly, as it may have calmed our nerves but would fail to address the ultimate source of the problem: POSSD. It was getting worse and worse by the day. Then one night, my husband came into the bedroom and said to me, "This has to end." The way he said "end." There was a finality to it. A permanence. I knew what he meant. This had to end for good. POSSD had to be stopped. By any means necessary. And there was no other way to make him stop in my mind than by having him, as they say in these upper-middle-class social circles, "taken care of and removed."

I know it sounds crazy, but I think I was beginning to acknowledge the impact my own traumatic past had on me and I was reminded of the cycles of abuse, constant fear, helplessness, and hopelessness. I became desperate for my own safety to return, but also my daughter, grandson, and all other parties directly involved. And medical issues caused many sleepless nights. I became blinded by reality causing me to no longer be logical and/or rational.

In that state of panic, I asked myself: How the hell does someone hire a hitman? And then I had an idea. One of my former patients was indebted to me, crediting me for restoring his life. I helped him find a way to function in the world again without feeling like his life was ruined. He was deeply grateful for my clinical skills and stated multiple times, "If there is anything you ever need, anything, no matter what it is, just ask me." I took that offer to heart.

I never thought my family would be faced with this terrifying state-of-affairs with no possibility of relief, and when I felt it was my responsibility to make things better, he listened as I explained the situation. Ten minutes passed between phone calls and then I saw a message from him: "I will help you." What felt like an eternity but was only a few days later, my former patient told me an associate of his would be contacting me. Jay was a "hitman" who agreed to do the task because he was doing my former patient a favor. Now the only question was, how much does something like this cost?

In my mind it seemed like POSSD was a red-light special. Not having done this before, when Jay suggested 10K plus 1K for expenses since he would need to drive to Florida, I agreed. Jay and I arranged to meet so I could provide the down payment, which my father gave me. Jay suggested a Walmart parking lot at an agreed upon time. He would find my car in the parking lot. The decision had been made, the plans all in place. It was October 30th, and we were ready.

My husband and I casually met friends for dinner at a restaurant in the local mall. No one had an inkling as to what was going to happen the following day. When we got home that night, I remember being quiet and pensive. We got into bed and as we lay there, I held my husband's hand and told him that I had a bad feeling. "Maybe we should not do this." Confidently, my husband remarked, "No one knows except us. No one knows but you, me, your dad, and Jay." "I know. I just have a bad feeling, like I'm going to get caught." "You're not going to get caught," my husband assured me. Still, I had a sixth sense. "In case I do get caught, I'm not taking you with me. Someone must be here to look after Alexis and Eli. If I get caught, I'm going down alone." Of course, my husband agreed.

When the morning came, Alexis saw the disposable phone her father had picked up for me to use. She became inquisitive, and I snapped it was none of her business. Then I went about my day. I was not nervous anymore. I suppose it was the calm before the storm.

The next day was Halloween. My husband was having breakfast at a diner with Alexis and Eli. On my way to meet "Jay," I stopped to pick up my unsweetened trenta green tea, light ice, from Starbucks. I filled my car up with gas and drove to the to Walmart or to the infamous life changing Walmart parking lot. There were a few cars there, but I did not see any police cars. I parked along the guardrail thinking it would give me better access if someone were watching me. And I waited. I was thinking of peace, family laughing together, joy, everything I was currently missing but craving. I could bring that back. I could save everyone.

There was a knock on my passenger window, and Jay got in and shut the door. I opened the FedEx envelope that had my husband's name and office address on it. I asked Jay to take the bills, all in hundreds, as I had already wiped them down. I handed him the money, which he accepted. He looked at me and said, "Are you sure you want to go through with it?" "Couldn't you just hurt him so he can't hurt anyone, no more children or women?" I asked. Jay responded, "I don't leave witnesses." And then I thought: I am a witness. But if I am going to die, I am taking POSSD with me. I have already had a great life; it would be worth it. Reluctantly, I told myself everything will be okay.

Jay continued to discuss the plan and asked me if I needed proof. I told him I was not sure. He said, "I could show you it's all done through Snapchat. Ten seconds and then the photo disappears without a trace." Then I got nervous. I asked, "What are you going to do with the body?" He looked at me, puzzled, he might have shrugged. In my anxiety, with sarcasm getting the best of me, I said, "You're doing this in Florida. Throw it to the gators."

And of all the things I said, this was the comment that went national, international, and would come back to haunt me for the rest of my life.

Jay shook my hand, left my car, and drove off. The business transaction was done. And I thought to myself, I cannot do this. Who am I? The transaction was already completed. It was out of my control. I could not stop it now. As I was driving away, I looked in the rearview mirror and saw a lot of police cars. Believe it or not, I thought they were going after somebody else— I was not speeding, I did not run any red lights. I pulled over for the officers to pass me, but they did not. I became very confused.

I still did not think this had anything so do with the actions just transpired. I rolled down the window. There were several officers surrounding me. The female officer asked me to get out of my car. "Can you please tell me why you pulled me over?" I asked. "We believe a crime was about to be committed." How could they know? No one knew, other than my husband, who got me the burner phone, and my dad, who sent me the money. Neither of them would have turned me in. But the police knew and arrested me immediately.

It turned out that my former patient, who might have recognized that I was in an insane and wildly uncontrolled state-of-mind, had turned me in. In the ten minutes it took him to text "I will help you" he had phoned the authorities, who sent an undercover agent to pose as "Jay the hitman" to see how far I would go. Clearly, I went too far and because no one tried to stop me or intervene I was in a serious predicament. The entire situation could have been avoided had the police still served and protected.

The rest is a bit of a blur. The police cuffed my hands behind my back and drove me to the police station. I had to surrender my purse, iPhone, burner phone and car keys. I was polite, cooperative and very naïve the whole way. When I got there, they placed me in a small office with a desk, where I sat alone. Finally, someone burst in. "I suggest you don't concoct any stories, as everything has been recorded," he said. "Jay, the so-called hitman, is a detective." I was stunned, and scared, and even though no one had read me my Miranda rights, I wanted to explain myself. I thought if I told the whole truth they would understand why I did what I did. That there was no other solution. Wouldn't any parent would do the same if they felt their child was in danger? I truly had no idea the severity of what I had done.

I said to him, "You wouldn't protect my daughter and my grandson, but I did." I told him the whole story about POSSD. The abuse. The fear. The threats to steal Eli and move him to Peru, the chatter on social media. I told him how POSSD threatened with his fists at days-old Eli's stomach when he cried, saying, "If you don't quit crying I'll punch you in the belly," or how he emotionally tortured my daughter from the moment he found out she was pregnant, how he even protested an emergency C-section because it would be too expensive: if the baby did not make it so what. I told him POSSD abandoned my daughter in every way including bullying her. I told him I suspected he raped Alexis, how her body froze in terror now when touched, especially near her neck, and that had never been the case before she got involved with POSSD. POSSD had even starved and abused the dogs, who came to me cowering and emaciated. I told him how POSSD refused to be present for the birth, refused to pay for diapers, refused to be a father in any way at all, yet said he was going to kidnap Eli so his mother would never see him again. I explained that my daughter is not the first woman to suffer at the hands of POSSD, that I had spoken to the mother of his other children who confirmed this. I told him that even POSSD's father agreed he was dangerous and helped us get Alexis and Eli out of the house while POSSD was out of town. I told him the truth: I had no other way to protect my family. He said, "We all have to protect our kids, but we don't have to break the law."

Bail was set at $250,000 or $500,000 bond. OJ Simpson's bail was also $500,000, and hc is a vicious, violent, cold-blooded murderer. He is a psychopath. Am I a violent cold-blooded murderer too? Am I a psychopath? Maybe I am. Or maybe I was pushed to a point of no return. Maybe, had the law enforcement or therapeutic systems recognized that my family was in imminent danger, that I was increasingly unstable, maybe they would have helped. Maybe I would not have done the unthinkable. Nevertheless, they are not to blame. I am the one who committed the crime. I am like OJ Simpson, it seems. I am the monster. My husband at the time knew everything, but did nothing to protect me.

Three hours later I was shackled for my arraignment. I collapsed outside the courtroom.

# CHAPTER 1: THE DREAM

It feels so good to drive the Mini-Cooper again, even though it is not the one I had grown to love driving several years earlier. This one is different, white and clean, with that new car and coffee smell, a USB port instead of a CD player. No one is in the passenger's seat. I am finally alone. I pull into my driveway and ease up that familiar incline, the one with the curve at the top of the landing. It has been so many years, but everything on the outside looks exactly as I remember. We had been lucky that winter. The weather did not seem too harsh on our property, and you could still see the signs of life in the grass. That green ribbon was still tied around our next-door neighbor's tree out in front. Jill, my next-door neighbor, tied a green ribbon around the tree the day I was sentenced. The gardens grew healthy and lush, transforming the driveway into a spectacular entrance, welcoming me home.

But I do not have a key. I go to the side garage door, hoping the spare house key is still under the Limoncello bottle in the garage freezer. It is! It is so comforting to know that when the world turns upside down, some things never change. I unlock the door when Marlin, an aging, impatient but very happy Bichon Friese, barrels out of the kitchen with such gusto I have to laugh. I am unsure if he knows he is a dog. Marlin is doing everything possible for me to know the cue to pick him up. He is five years older than the was the last time I saw him. He was my birthday present and I always treated him like my baby. Marlin begins to bark, then ups the ante to an excited whine. He missed me as much as I missed him. He gives me a good thorough sniffing before walking back into the house with me—has my scent changed that much? I would not know. All I know is that this is my house, my home. It feels indescribably good to be back.

As I look around I realize things look different—so much has been removed. Where did all the coats and shoes go that were in the mud room? Where did the dog leashes go? And the pictures...the walls are now a solid light green where once photos and souvenirs were proudly and tastefully displayed. I do not even see the outline where the frames and shelves used to be. It appears the past has been erased as if I never existed. I continue to walk into the kitchen and down the long hallway into our bedroom. Nothing on the walls there either. My "Boudoir" photo canvas has been taken down, and that spot where I had painted a caricature of my husband and me, with our smiles too broad and our goofy expressions hyper extended, that's gone, painted over as well.

I am sitting in the rocking chair in my old bedroom crying. I have no home and am exhausted from my drive. I am overwhelmed by being in the house that I called home. I can't find anything and see nothing familiar. And I can feel it now, my inner clock tells me that 4 P.M. is closing in. Almost time for Count in Taconic. I am not there anymore. Maybe I did develop some institutionalized issues. I check my watch. Was coming back home really a good idea? I do not have many minutes left before show time. Time to prepare…

I remove all my outer clothing to reveal a black lace push-up bra, lacy thong and black fishnet stockings affixed to a black garter belt with tiny pink bows. From my purse, I remove my favorite pumps. I always loved the snakeskin heel and the patent leather shoe together. I wiggle my foot into the casings, and it feels so right. It has been too long since I sported sexy shoes. I look in the mirror for reassurance: Hair, check. Makeup, not too trashy and perfect. I still got it. I am good to go. It is showtime!

I walk back into the living room and sit in what we casually refer to as the A.D.D. seat. It is the kind of upholstered chair that swivels and rocks, perfect for people who struggle to pay attention and need repetitive motion to help them self soothe. It's fair to say that when I was a licensed practicing therapist, the vast majority of my patients suffered from some form of Attention Deficit Disorder. Maybe this chair would have helped them. Marlin makes a beeline for my lap, refusing to wait another second. It is as if he had been practicing while I was gone to win a gold medal in dog kisses. I really missed my furry boy: It feels so good to be able to rub Marlin's ears and his soft spotted pink belly while I admire my dress shoes and swivel in my seat and wait for 4:00.

Suddenly Marlin, my smart dog jumps off my lap and prepares to greet my ex-husband. Some things never change. He begins to whine as I listen. My ex-husband is pulling into the driveway: I hear the garage door open, then close. I hear a key turning in the door, and then the door opens, and he is here. He is placing his wallet and keys on a shelf above the desk as he always does. And then he sees me, and he gasps, "Melisa! What are you doing here? This is not your house anymore." I smile seductively. "How was your day, dear?" My husband nervously asks, "Did you escape? I am calling the police." I smirk and respond, "No need to call the police. I have that covered." Several federal agents suddenly appear and surround my ex-husband. These cops are not playing around. This is good, karma is a bitch. One of the agents tells him to put his hands behind his back, while another reads him his rights. He has the right to remain silent. He has the right to an attorney. Plastic zip-tie handcuffs enclose his wrists, which are firmly hoisted behind him. I happen to know that hurts, and I am glad. My ex-husband wails, "Melisa, why would you do this to me? I am the father of your children. We had a deal." Some deal. I tell the agents to take him away. As my ex-husband (father of my children) leaves my sight…I finally exhale and breathe.

Just then, my eyes open. I take my time, I feel disoriented reaquainting myself with a room smaller than my bathroom or a room that is 8 x 6 feet. The paint is old and chipped, a stale sweaty smell has replaced the aroma from the garden. I cannot find my high-heeled shoes; a dark green uniform has obscured my sexy lingerie, and Marlin has disappeared. I have awakened from this dream again and again and I am still here. I am still at Taconic Correctional Facility in Bedford Hills, New York, serving my sentence.

I get it now. I attempted to hire a hitman to kill my daughter's abusive boyfriend. I thought I could prevent him from following through on his scary promises and punish him for his heinous behavior. I was and still am terrified (he or POSSD) could potentially do the same thing he did to my grandson's older siblings. I am guilty as charged, and I belong here. I do not feel like I am a victim, and even though I am in prison and that recurring dream is just a torturous fantasy of how justice might have really been served, prison is only geography. I am free in every way that matters. I am freer than I have ever been.

# Chapter 2: Bitter

Before this all started, I thought I had a great life. My husband at the time and I were adapting to life as empty nesters. We were living in what I thought was our forever dream home on the lake. At the time, in my mind we worked hard together to get to where we were at this stage in our life. Looking back, I was fooling myself. My daughter and her baby needed help and like any parent we helped her. I am her mother and at the time, my daughter was in trouble. Parents protect their children. As a new grandmother I had double the responsibility. However, it was horrifying to think that my daughter felt just as scared and hopeless about the situation as I did. I feared for her and my grandson's safety.

It is terrifying to imagine POSSD with children—from the moment Eli was born, POSSD treated him and Alexis with contempt and non-physical abuse, which can be more dangerous than physical abuse. He did not even bring her to the hospital when she was in labor, my brother happened to call at the right time and drove her. When POSSD finally showed up, she had been having contractions for several hours. He would roll his eyes and tell her to not to be so dramatic. The nurse tried to provide comic relief when she asked him if he ever had a grape come out of his penis. He left as soon as she got the epidural, because he was annoyed that she wanted one. He would not even acknowledge that I was there when I offered to help. He got bored, he said he was going back home to sleep. When I called to tell him she needed a C-section, he argued that she did not need one, and refused to pay (as if he were going to pay for anything). As soon as the baby was cleaned off and Alexis was in the recovery room he left. I felt all alone and had no idea what to do for myself or my daughter.

I got Alexis flowers. I signed up for the picture package. POSSD made my daughter feel like she was a huge inconvenience. And she was scared to death of him. She knew how violent and abusive he could be. It took him 24 hours to come and see her again. Ten hours after Eli was born he was admitted to the PICU for antibiotics due to a high white blood cell count. I remember Alexis telling him this over the phone and her feeling like her body failed at keeping her baby safe. POSSD insisted it was not necessary and would be more money. When Alexis asked when he was coming I over heard him say, "I'll be there…hour or so." They lived 10 minutes from the hospital. POSSD returned to the hospital that night, after Alexis had already left her room to go to PICU to feed Eli.

During a time where love and joy should have surrounded us, POSSD was a menace. I could not handle how Alexis and Eli were being treated. My hurt turned into anger. When my husband tried to say anything positive about the situation, I became angrier and eventually more distant. I found the pain and the isolation terrifying and I felt abandoned and neglected all over again. I never wanted my daughter to experience what I did throughout my complicated relationship with my own mother, who had passed away 5 years before Eli was born. This was never what I had envisioned for my children or for us as grandparents. I could not let Alexis see the impact the dynamics or lack of dynamics were having on me; I searched the hospital for a chapel. It had been a long time since God had heard my voice. I needed some help. I needed a great amount of help. But I could not find the chapel and out of frustration and exhaustion I just collapsed against a wall while sobbing on the phone to my husband.

Her home was worse than the hospital. POSSD did not want Alexis breastfeeding, and he'd find every way to sabotage her. He did not want her breastmilk to be in a baby bottle either; he'd add cereal and cut off the top of the bottle nipples. It was okay, in POSSD's eyes, if Eli was choking, he'd have to "man up." He refused to have a Diaper Genie in the nursery and told Alexis that she could go up and down the stairs and dispose of the diapers in the kitchen garbage. Not only is that disgusting, Alexis had a C-section and could barely walk.

From everything I had been told, POSSD was even more abusive to the mother of his other children. He would beat her regularly, abuse her mentally, and violate her sexually. And though she did not come out and say it, Alexis alluded that she had been sexually assaulted by him as well. When Alexis phoned home, ironically on Halloween crying again and asked if she could move home, of course we said yes.

There was a small window of opportunity, that day after Thanksgiving, as POSSD and his other kids were driving from Fort Lauderdale to Glen Cove. And my husband was on it. In order to accomplish this, a carefully coordinated plan took place. With the help of Alexis' close friends and family, a moving company that to this day I will never forget, how supportive they all were in making sure my child and her son were brought to a safe environment. Even the landlord, knowing what was going on, changed the locks on the door after they were gone. The day after Thanksgiving they arrived home, and my husband called POSSD to tell him that Alexis had moved out.

As usual, POSSD was verbally abusive to my husband, which only re-enforced the severity of the domestic situation. Alexis and Eli with their two dogs, Max and Bella, moved into our home. Bella looked like a rescue dog who had not been fed in months. She shuddered at the site of any construction tools. POSSD worked in construction. Max looked and acted like he had been thrown against a wall. It was all horrifying. What mattered is that my child was home and would be given an opportunity to raise her child without constant fear. I lived in an endless state of fear, resentment, and frustration.

Alexis was not the Alexis I used to know. My daughter was not this kind of persnickety, snarky girl prior to this relationship with POSSD, and I resented her behavior. At the same time, I was worried about her. When I went to hug her and she did not see it coming, she jumped, frightened to death. I could not touch her neck or shoulders without her becoming rigid and looking like she was saying her final goodbyes.

The dogs were traumatized. Bella was so emaciated I could see her pelvis and all her ribs. As a puppy, she has required half a dozen surgeries and a feeding tube, after attempting to consume a shoe. All food had to be liquified. During that time, Bella became my BFF. My new job was to fatten her up. Now, an adult dog, she weighed seventeen pounds when she arrived. She should have weighed at least twenty-seven pounds. She would not stop trembling, so we wound up buying her a Thunder-Shirt to reduce anxiety, something dogs wear during a bad storm. Bella wore it every day for three months.

Who knew how all of this would trigger me and intensify my own traumatic experiences from my past? How can one man impact every aspect of so many others?

# CHAPTER 3: MAMA BEAR

POSSD was not out of the picture. He would call and text Alexis endlessly, sometimes hundreds of times a day. He wanted pictures of her breastfeeding, pictures of her dressed up as a school- girl with her hair in pigtails. He wanted pictures of her naked, squirting breastmilk at him. She told him not to call or text, but he was relentless. He said he was going to come and take Eli. Alexis called the local police. They came over, filled out a report, called POSSD, instructed him to stop. POSSD would be ever so polite with the police, but then he would resume the incessant messages, borrowing someone else's phone, creating a different social media account, anything he could devise to harass her. Clearly the words from the police had no meaning. At one point I called POSSD on the phone and begged him to just leave Alexis alone. He mocked me.

Alexis was so broken and fragile; it was more than she could handle. She was a great mother, but I could tell she was not taking care of herself. As her mother I felt that I needed to take care of my daughter. She was not a kid, but she was still my child. I would take Eli for regular walks, I fed her dogs; though I worked three to four days a week I still cooked, cleaned, ran errands. I tried to talk to her, which was difficult because I was so emotional, so I had to speak to her clinically in order to help. But it was almost impossible for me to stay calm, and she was in a rage, throwing her stuff everywhere, which she knew would drive me nuts. Often, I would get in my car and drive around and find a place to park and just sob.

Finally, I said to her, "What is the problem, why are you so angry and why are you doing this?" "I'm the family fuckup, that's the role Dad assigned me, and you went along." "Why do you think that?" "Because it's true." I realized, for the first time, that I was the only person who ever protected her. I made it my mission to make things better. Perhaps I had codependency traits and thought I always had to make things better even if it meant being a mama bear? I had made her feel inadequate and incompetent.

Meanwhile, she was getting on my nerves. Why couldn't she just pick up after herself? I could not deal with all her purses and parcels living in my kitchen. We had a baby in the house, why couldn't she just take off her shoes? Why was I the one washing the dog paws? Why didn't she have enough respect for me to live in my home politely? I hated my washer and dryer in constant use—can't you please hang the clothes outside to dry instead, as I have asked numerous times, because it makes them smell good and reduces our carbon footprint? I would feel rage when Alexis would do the laundry at midday, and then throw everything in the dryer. I began to feel offended if anything was left out of place, or not returned to its location. I became truly anal retentive, putting away things obsessively and flipping out when things were in disorder.

Over the next two years, POSSD never let up. I was grateful Alexis connected with the other "baby mama." What they say is true, two mothers are better than the FBI. When it came to protecting all four of POSSD's children, both Alexis and Eli's siblings' mother utilized their intelligence and pooled their resources. Together they figured out POSSD's social media passwords. The other mom translated Spanish messages exchanged back and forth amongst a friend of his mother's who still lived in Peru. He was allegedly going to marry her and the plan according to their research indicated the woman was excited to come to America or stay in Peru and raise all the children. She even stated in messages, "I can't wait to hold the baby." I found out from Alexis that POSSD was granted custody of the twins who at the time were in their early teens. This terrified me and I began to think that if I didn't protect Alexis, the other mom, and all the kids, POSSD would continue this pattern with someone else and continue to remain unscathed.

August 2014 would be POSSD's only supervised visit. I was convinced that this would be one of the many supervised visits POSSD would be having with Eli in the near future. Alexis's attorney suggested having the visit in a familiar place supervised by people Eli was well acquainted with. It made sense to have the visit at Poppy's office in the waiting room. At first I was repulsed, resentful, and irate that our life had to be put on hold because POSSD felt like visiting. When my husband forbade me from going to the office, I harbored resentment that never seemed to ease up. I suppose he was afraid of what I would say or do, but I have never done well with orders. Yet I was the dutiful wife and remained at home, growing more resentful and terrified with each minute POSSD was with Eli.

The visit went well. This was crushing any hope of my grandson having a normal childhood. If POSSD was successful in his attendance and behavior over four supervised visits, the court would grant him permission to take Eli alone for a week. Would he beat him? Steal him? There was no way of knowing. And he was still harassing Alexis. She continued to file complaints; the police would come to our house again and again. They would ask the same question "What kind of threat is it?" They would tell Alexis, "Get a different phone number and change your email address." Seeing the frustration Alexis was experiencing over and over made me frustrated and angry. I asked myself, why does the victim have to be the one to make the changes. How does POSSD get to stay below the radar without consequences for his actions.

Alexis turned to the justice system to limit POSSD's rights as a parent, stressing his abusive history. But the courts gave him more and more privileges. I don't think she was taken seriously by the imminent danger POSSD presented to my family—no one looked into his past violent history nor did they interview POSSD's other baby mama or the three children that he had hurt and abused. I considered exposing this, but I was also deeply afraid that if I reported everything about POSSD to the police, they would call Child Protective Services. Eli would be removed from our home and placed into foster care while an investigation took place. As a licensed clinical social worker with a well established private practice in the community, I had first hand knowledge of the horrors that frequently happen when a child is removed and placed in the foster care system. This is not to say there are not good placements as well.

My fears spiraled and I became completely consumed by them. This combined with chronic pain turned into violent nightmares, which morphed into insomnia, which I preferred to the torture of my dreams. I would stay up all night and worry obsessively about Alexis and Eli: Eli, a gentle, kind, intelligent boy, would be turned into a defiant, perhaps even a violent, resentful kid. I believed he would hate his mother, his poppy and me for letting his abusive, bully, biological father spend time alone with him. Aside from that, where was POSSD all those nights that Eli was awake and one of us was walking with him while he cried? Where was POSSD at the register when we had to pay for diapers and formula? POSSD might get Eli alone for a week? Unfathomable. This was not a dad. He was a very dangerous man who happened to be my grandson's biological father.

Professionally, I know the effects of not sleeping. My mind and body were no longer in sync. I was always fighting or fleeing. Sleep deprivation is a form of incremental torture. When the mind, body, and spirit breaks down, it can develop psychosis. After five straight days and nights, this is exactly what happened to me. I could not do anything except fixate on POSSD and keeping Alexis and Eli safe. In the hours after midnight I became more vigilant and more desperate about everything. What if he took Eli and moved to Peru? What if he beat Eli and turned him into a monster? What if the fist he put to Eli's belly when he was five days old was a predictor of fists to come? What if my daughter died because she could not take it anymore? What if there was no end to this, and Alexis was going to live with us permanently? What if Eli could never acclimate in school—the signs were there. When Eli was nine months old, Alexis found a daycare provider to watch him so she could substitute teach.   By the third day, she had to resign. Eli was inconsolable and upsetting the other children. What if POSSD came to our house in a rage? What if he took my child and my grandchild and beat them to death? I went to a very dark place.

# CHAPTER 4: FULL COURT PRESS

**New York Woman Wanted Grandson's Father Dead,
Body Thrown to the Alligators, Authorities Say**

—By MARA SCHIAVOCAMPO, ABC NEWS 2014

A grandmother and social worker in upstate New York has been accused in a murder-for-hire plot, planning to have her grandson's father killed and his body fed to alligators, authorities say.

Melisa Schonfield, 57, was arrested Friday after she allegedly tried to hire a hitman to kill NAME REDACTED of Florida for $11,000. Schonfield's daughter and NAME REDACTED have a 2-year-old together.

Schonfield met Jefferson County Sheriff's Det. Dave Pustizzi inside her car at a Walmart in Watertown, New York, according to court documents. He was posing as the would-be hitman.

Schonfield said the best way to get rid of the body would be to "throw it to the alligators," according to the detective.

The accusations shocked Schonfield's daughter, Alexis, 31, who found out about the arrest on Facebook. Alexis Schonfield said NAME REDACTED has been verbally abusive to her. ABC News attempted to contact NAME REDACTED but he could not be reached for comment.

Alexis Schonfield said her mother has not admitted to doing anything wrong, only that she loves her daughter.

"This only happens on a *Lifetime* movie, you know?" Alexis Schonfield said in an exclusive interview with ABC News. "My mom is not a monster."

Alexis Schonfield also rejected allegations that her father, a well-known dentist, was aware of his wife's alleged plans.

Schonfield is home on bail, charged with second-degree conspiracy and criminal solicitation. She has pleaded not guilty, her lawyer said. Schonfield isn't alone in allegedly plotting to have a loved one killed. Indeed, trying to hire someone to make a loved one disappear is more common than you think. The motives often include money, broken hearts and revenge.

### Man in Murder-For-Hire Alligator Case Was Targeted Before (Exclusive)
—By David Lohr, HuffPo, 2014

NAME REDACTED, the man whose ex-girlfriend's mom is accused of plotting to hire a hitman to kill him and feed his body to alligators, was marked for violence earlier by the husband of another ex-girlfriend, according to authorities. NAME REDACTED, who said he did nothing to inspire the contract murder plot police said they broke up last week, was attacked three years ago by the pistol-wielding husband of an ex-girlfriend, authorities said. The husband clubbed NAME REDACTED twice on the head with a .38-caliber pistol and a shot was fired during their struggle, police said. NAME REDACTED was treated for head wounds. The husband awaits trial on an assault charge. "He came to kill me," NAME REDACTED told HuffPost. "He attacked me with a gun and everything. It got ugly and I defended myself."

NAME REDACTED was the focus of violence again on Oct. 31, when police arrested Melisa Rae Schonfield, 57, a social worker from

Brownville, New York, after she allegedly paid a down payment on NAME REDACTED's murder to an undercover detective posing as a hitman. Schonfield, mother of NAME REDACTED's most recent ex-girlfriend, Alexis Schonfield, with whom NAME REDACTED has a child, is free on bail charged with second-degree conspiracy and second-degree criminal solicitation. Neither ex-girlfriend is implicated in the charges. Both said in interviews with HuffPost that NAME REDACTED was abusive to them. NAME REDACTED denied abusing either woman and authorities filed no charges suggesting he did. He acknowledged he was subject to a protection from abuse order with his first ex-girlfriend, but said it had nothing to do with violence. While it's not uncommon for ex- boyfriends to incite anger in relatives of ex-girlfriends, it may be unheard of for the same individual to inspire lethal intentions in two unrelated cases, according to an expert who specializes in criminal cases. "I can only speculate, but for the [family members] to be that angry, they must have perceived some real danger and hazard to their [loved ones] from this man," Dr. Rona M. Fields told HuffPost. Fields, author of eight books, is an internationally recognized authority on domestic violence and neuropsychology. She is the former president of the District of Columbia Psychological Association and has been practicing clinical psychology in the Washington area since 1977. Fields said she was "all but certain" both families "were probably frustrated and deeply grieved by what had happened to these women." Fatima Del Toro, who has three children with NAME REDACTED, declined to discuss the charges against her husband, Ramon Colindres, 40. According to court records, Colindres went after NAME REDACTED with a loaded .38 Special on Nov. 13, 2011, in the parking lot of the Florida apartment complex where NAME REDACTED lived. "Let's see how tough you are now," Colindres said, according to the police affidavit. "Ramon Colindres then struck NAME REDACTED with the gun twice, on the top of the head," the affidavit states. "The second time NAME REDACTED was struck with the gun, a round went off." A struggle ensued and the pistol was lost under a nearby car. Police broke up the fight. NAME REDACTED was treated for his injuries and Colindres was arrested for aggregated battery with a firearm "in a way likely to produce death," the complaint says. Colindres' lawyer, Fred Haddad, of Fort Lauderdale, Florida, said he doesn't believe his client did "anything improperly." "He was acting properly in response to what was occurring to him and the family," Haddad told HuffPost on Friday. "There's not much more I can say." Colindres' trial is likely to be held in the next few weeks. Del Toro said her husband's arrest followed her 14-year relationship with NAME REDACTED that produced three children. "I started dating him when I was 14," Del Toro told HuffPost. "I was 15 when he became very abusive— physically, verbally and mentally. There was no way to tell anyone, so I hid it." Del Toro said she left him in 2008. "It got to the point where he would say we would be a statistic on TV—that he would kill me and the kids," she said. "What actually did it for me was when we were driving over a bridge by where we lived and he said he was going to drive the car off the bridge and we were going to die—all of us. My kids were screaming, and my son cried for his stuffed animal to save him. He was holding onto it and said, 'Please save me, please save me.' It's one of those things that will never leave me." Del Toro said NAME REDACTED stalked her after she left him, and she got two restraining orders against him. "Even after I left, I would come out of work and he would be sitting there," she said. "He would even come into my apartment building in the middle of the night. It got to the point that I had to move in with my parents." According to Broward County court records, a protection against violence order was granted in August 2008 and was valid until February 2009. A second order, granted in June 2009, was valid until June 2010. Del Toro's abuse allegations are "all false," NAME REDACTED said. "She's weird. It's a big drama. All I wanted was my kids and it turned into this big issue." NAME REDACTED acknowledged one of the restraining orders, but said it was "part of the process that [the courts] put you through." He added: "They didn't want me to come near her.

She wanted me to have supervised visitation and I told her that was crazy." Del Toro's brother, Moises Del Toro, said his family is frustrated that NAME REDACTED "is going to portray himself out to be the victim." "We went through a lot of things with him," Moises Del Toro said. "We have a whole family willing to go on record. He manipulates, abuses and threatens people. These are not people who are crazy or anything. They got pushed to the extreme. He never stops. He keeps coming and coming and coming." NAME REDACTED said Moises Del Toro's allegations are "completely false." "He's being an idiot," NAME REDACTED said. "He's always harassing me."

In the latest case, a tipster in Jefferson County, New York, alerted authorities that Melisa Schonfield was looking for a hitman to take out NAME REDACTED, according to the sheriff's department. An undercover detective posing as a hired killer met Melisa Schonfield in the parking lot of a Watertown Walmart on Halloween. Schonfield agreed to pay $11,000 for the rubout, according to police, and suggested the best way to dispose of the body would be to "throw it to the alligators." She was taken into custody after giving the undercover officer a $5,500 down payment, police said. Authorities haven't revealed a motive. Jefferson County District Attorney Cindy Intschert declined to discuss the case. Alexis Schonfield, 31, was hesitant to discuss the charges against her mom, but said her "on and off again" relationship with NAME REDACTED was volatile. "The only thing I can say, because I am a mother, is she was trying to protect my son and she got tired of watching me cry," Schonfield said. "I've been an emotional basket case the past two years." Alexis Schonfield said she began dating NAME REDACTED in Florida after his split with Del Toro. "Looking back, it was probably almost immediately that I noticed something was off," Schonfield said. "He and Fatima would fight a lot over the phone. He made it sound like she was this horrible woman. He always yelled and screamed at her. You couldn't even make sense of it. I just thought she was provoking him, because that's what he told me." Schonfield and she left NAME REDACTED in November 2012, when their child was 3 months old. "I called my dad hysterical and said I got to get outta here. We planned it for Thanksgiving because [NAME REDACTED] was going to Long Island to visit family." Schonfield said NAME REDACTED "went back and forth between him being really nice and him calling me crazy names and accusing me of ridiculous things." "It was the same thing over and over again and I didn't want my son to have to worry about saying the wrong thing or doing the wrong thing," she said.

NAME REDACTED claimed Schonfield "is not mentally stable." "That's why me and Alexis broke up," he said. "She was so up and down and I couldn't handle that. I can see it in her face—you can tell when someone's not there and she's not there—she's crazy. Her mom's the same way." NAME REDACTED said he sees a link between the alleged murder-for-hire plot and the 2011 assault. "I know for a fact these people all know each other and are friends," he said. "Last year I came across this one picture on Facebook where all of them went out to dinner. That kind of spooks me. I have a gut feeling that there's some link there. I can't prove it, but I'm pretty sure."

Del Toro and Alexis Schonfield said they keep in contact so their children can have a relationship, but denied conspiring against NAME REDACTED. "Absolutely not," Schonfield said. "We're not in cahoots with any of this. What my mom allegedly did was wrong, but she had two women—her daughter and this other woman that she has grown to love like a daughter—and she didn't want this to go on anymore." Both Schonfield and Del Toro said they sought help at various times during their relationships with NAME REDACTED, to no avail. Del Toro said she called the police in 1997 or 1998 "about a domestic violence issue." But she said NAME REDACTED told police that Del Toro hit him as well, she said, "so the cop said we had to let it go or we would both get arrested for domestic abuse." Alexis Schonfield said she was told she was unable to get a restraining order against NAME REDACTED. "I don't know how to explain it, other than he knows how to stay just under the legal radar," Schonfield said. "He knows how to do enough without overdoing it."

For now, both families—and NAME REDACTED—await the criminal justice system's movement. "It's like a *Lifetime* movie," Schonfield said. "You wouldn't believe it if you weren't living it."

## WHY DO THIS GUY'S GIRLFRIENDS WANT HIM DEAD

> – January 16th, 2015. By Lucy C. LAWYERS and SETTLEMENTS.COM

It must have seemed like a good idea at the time. Or not. In any event, one 57-year-old social worker from Brownville, New York decided, she'd had enough—enough of her daughter's ex-boyfriend, and father of her two-year-old grandson, so she hired a hitman to kill him and feed him to the crocodiles. (Would I make this up?) Luckily for the ex—the "hitman" turned out to be an undercover detective and mamma has been arrested and charged with both second-degree criminal solicitation and conspiracy in the second degree.

Melisa Rae Schonfield tried to hire Detective Dave Pustizzi to kill NAME REDACTED, a resident of Florida. Pustizzi was also supposed to be the one serving NAME REDACTED to the crocs. Nothing vague about those intentions.

Apparently, a tipster gave the Jefferson County Sheriff's Department a heads up about Melisa Schonfield's plans. "We got a tip from a concerned citizen," Detective Dave Pustizzi told HuffPost. According to court documents, Schonfield met the undercover detective posing as a hitman at a Walmart parking lot in Watertown. What is it with Walmart parking lots?

### Crazy sh*t lawyers see

Schonfield had the readies—she agreed to pay the undercover detective $11,000 for NAME REDACTED's murder, according to police. She suggested the best way to dispose of the body would be to "throw it to the alligators," police said. She told the supposed contract killer that her husband, a Watertown dentist, was aware of what she was doing and "even made a smart remark about her getting caught," according to the court documents. Mrs. Schonfield was taken into custody after giving the undercover officer a $5,500 down payment, police said. I wonder what the fee was for feeding the crocs? Of note, neither the daughter or her father have been implicated in the attempted "hit."

Needless to say, NAME REDACTED is shocked, and Alexis Schonfield—the ex- girlfriend—is also equally stunned.

"It's just f–ked up," 36-year-old NAME REDACTED told The Huffington Post in an exclusive interview. "I don't know why she would want to kill me. I haven't spoken to her in a long time." Maybe that's why....

NAME REDACTED and Alexis parted company in 2012, reportedly, with Alexis moving to New York with their young son. NAME REDACTED stayed in Florida—in retrospect—not such a bad idea.

According to HuffPo, NAME REDACTED said he had no recent issues with anyone in the family. "I wasn't fighting" for custody, he said. "It was already settled."

As for the murder plot, he said, "I have no idea why. I can't believe she went this far." Ah—just how far would have been acceptable?

"The only thing I can say, because I am a mother, is she was trying to protect my son and she got tired of watching me cry," 31-year-old Alexis said. "I've been an emotional basket case the past two years." Had anyone thought of therapy?

But here's the kicker—Alexis said she learned of her mother's arrest on Facebook. Seriously. "I had no idea what was going on," she said. "I thought she was going to go visit her friends in Rochester over the weekend. When I found out, I was in shock." Bet the friends in Rochester are relieved.

Schonfield said her "on and off again "relationship with NAME REDACTED was volatile. "I think emotional and verbal domestic abuse is a big joke to people … [but] it's just as bad as physical violence," she said. "It's just that the scars are not visible," she told HuffPo.

There's a weird twist here, though, which is that this is not the first time NAME REDACTED has allegedly inspired someone to want to kill him. Three years ago he was attacked by the pistol-wielding husband of yet another an ex-girlfriend, according to HuffPo. The husband clubbed NAME REDACTED twice on the head with a .38-caliber pistol and a shot was fired during their struggle, police said. NAME REDACTED was treated for head wounds. The not-so-lucky husband is reportedly awaiting trial on an assault charge. Has anyone here heard of talk therapy?

"He came to kill me," NAME REDACTED told HuffPost. "He attacked me with a gun and everything. It got ugly and I defended myself."

While we might be tempted to think this guy is either very unlucky or has some really bad juju going on, NAME REDACTED sees it quite differently. In addition to being grateful to the police, he said, "God really looked out for me. He really did."

He feels sorry for Melisa Schonfield. "It didn't have to go this way— she didn't have to do what she did," he said. "She ruined her reputation and now there's no grandma in the picture for my son. I feel bad."

# CHAPTER 5: CRIME AND PUNISHMENT

IN COUNTY COURT COUNTY OF JEFFERSON

THE PEOPLE OF THE
STATE OF NEW YORK

-against-

MELISA R. SCHONFIELD
INDICTMENT

Indictment 630-14

Attempted Murder in the First Degree
Penal Law §110/125.27(1)(a)and (b)
Conspiracy in the Second Degree
Penal Law §105.15
Criminal Solicitation in the Second
Degree Penal Law §100.10
Cindy F. Intschert, Jefferson County
District Attorney A TRUE BILL

THE GRAND JURY OF THE COUNTY OF JEFFERSON, by this Indictment, accuses MELISA R. SCHONFIELD of the offense of ATTEMPTED MURDER IN THE FIRST DEGREE, in violation of Section 110/125.27(1)(a)(vi) and (b) of the Penal Law of New York State, connoted as follows:

That the said MELISA R. SCHONFIELD, on or about and during the month of October 2014, in the County of Jefferson and State of New York, being 18 years or older, attempted to intentionally cause the death of another person or third person and commit the killing or procured commission of the killing pursuant to an agreement with a person other than the intended victim to commit the same for the receipt, or in expectation of the receipt, of anything of pecuniary value from a party to the agreement or from a person other than the intended victim acting at the direction of a party to such agreement, to wit: the defendant being 18 years or older (DOB: September 21, 1957), attempted to intentionally cause the death of another, pursuant to an agreement with a person other than the intended victim, that the victim would be killed in exchange for monetary payment by the defendant.

SECOND COUNT

AND THE GRAND JURY AFORESAID, by a second count of this Indictment, further accuses the staid MELISA R. SCHONFIELD of the offense of CONSPIRACY IN THE SECOND DEGREE, in violation of Section 105.15 of the Penal Law of New York State, committed as follows:

That the said MELISA R. SCHONFIELD, on or about and during the month of October 2014, in the County of Jefferson and State of New York, with intent that conduct constituting a class A felony be performed, she agreed with one or more persons to engage in or cause the performance of such conduct, to wit: the defendant, with intent that murder in the second degree, a class A felony, be performed, agreed with another to engage in or cause the performance of such conduct, and in furtherance of said agreement provided money to another to induce him to cause the death of a third person.

## THIRD COUNT

AND THE GRAND JURY AFORESAID, by a third count of this Indictment, further accuses the said MELISA R. SCHONFIELD of the offense of CRIMINAL SOLICITATION IN THE SECOND DEGREE, in violation of Section 100.10 of the Penal Law of New York State, committed as follows:

That the said MELISA R. SCHONFIELD, on or about and during the month of October 2014, in the County of Jefferson and State of New York, with intent that another person engage in conduct constituting a class A felony, she solicited, requested, commanded, importuned or otherwise attempted to cause such other person to engage in such conduct, to wit: the defendant, with intent that another person engage in conduct constituting murder in the second degree, a class A felony, she solicited, requested, importuned or otherwise attempted to cause another to engage in such conduct.

## STATE OF NEW YORK COUNTY OF JEFFERSON COUNTY COURT

PEOPLE OF THE STATE OF NEW YORK

Index: 14-2067 Indictment: 630-14

-Against-

MELISA R. SCHONFIELD, Defendant,

WAIVER OF RIGHT TO APPEAL

My attorneys, Kimberly Zimmer and Emil Rossi, have advised me of my right to appeal from the plea of guilty and sentence agreed upon June 16111 20 15, convicting me of PL§l 10/125.25(1) and sentencing me to the following: Sentence to time left to the discretion of the Court (5 Years State Prison followed by 5 Years PRS per Court); NYSC; Forfeiture of moneys held as evidence in the case, WOA; DNA Fee; Crime Victim Fee. l have been informed that, unless waived, I have the right to appeal from the conviction that will result from this plea and that if I am unable to afford an attorney to represent me on appeal, one will be appointed. l do not wish to retain my right to appeal. I understand that by signing this document, I am agreeing to enter a guilty plea, and thereby waive my right to appeal from the above-mentioned plea and sentence on the following grounds:

(A) Sufficiency of the Indictment and the proof presented before the Grand Jury;

(B) Form and content of the Indictment or Information;

(C) The decision and order of the Court on any pre-trial motions made by the defendant;

(D) Voluntariness of any statements made by the defendant;

(E) Sufficiency of the plea allocution;

(F) Sentence;

(G) Any and all deportation, immigration, or other collateral consequences related to a guilty plea and sentence;

(H) Any other matters which may have an appeal as of right or otherwise.

I understand that this waiver is intended to be as broad as the law allows and encompasses all issues arising from this criminal proceeding and I certify that I am not under the influence of any drugs or alcohol or medication that prevents me from understanding the consequences of this waiver.

I understand that the right to appeal is separate and distinct from those rights that I have automatically forfeited upon my plea of guilty and that although I retain my right to appeal even after pleading guilty, I have been offered the plea stated above on the condition that I give up that right.

I understand that I am waiving my right to appeal knowingly, voluntarily and intelligently. I have had a full opportunity to discuss these matters with my attorney, and any questions I may have been answered to my satisfaction.

The above-named defendant appeared before this Court on this date and in open court, in the presence of this Court, and with the approval of this Court and with the advised attorney, signed the foregoing waiver of her right to appeal.

**The Sentencing**

THE COURT: Call the matter of Melisa Schonfield.

It is my understanding there is a proposed disposition. Mr. Shaffer, would you like to outline the proposal?

MR. SHAFFER: Yes, Your Honor.

In the matter of the People of the State of New York versus Melisa Schonfield, Indictment number—top count being Attempted Murder in the First Degree, it's my understanding that the defendant is prepared to enter a plea to Attempted Murder in the Second Degree with intent under New York State Penal Law Subdivision, which carries a potential sentencing range of between 5 and 30 years in state prison, followed by between two and a half to five years post-release supervision. This portion of the sentence is being left to the discretion of the Court.

The remainder of the plea offer is contingent upon forfeiture of money, and the two cell phones confiscated from the defendant in this case.

The plea offer is further conditioned upon a written Waiver of Appeal, New York State surcharge, DNA fee and a permanent stay-away Order of Protection for the victim.

It is the People's understanding the defendant has executed a written Waiver of Appeal and the forfeiture agreement including the cell phones and money. With that understanding, Your Honor, People would move to disposition at this time.

THE COURT: Mr. Rossi, is that your understanding of what we are going to be doing here today?

MR. ROSSI: Yes, with the exception, Judge, of the fact that we have discussed the proposed sentence and the determination has been made that the sentence will be five years imprisonment and five years post-release supervision.

THE COURT: Please swear the defendant.

COURT OFFICER: Please state and spell your name for the Court.

THE DEFENDANT: Melisa Rae Schonfield, M-e-l-i-s-a, R-a-e, S-c-h-o-n-f-i-e-l-d

THE COURT: Ms. Schonfield, I'm going to ask you a series of questions here today. You are now under oath, so your answers must be truthful. If they are not truthful, you could be charged with another crime called Perjury, so feel free to talk to either of your attorneys standing next to you any time you want to before you answer any of my questions. You have heard the outline of the proposed disposition here today. It's my understanding you are prepared to plead guilty to the amended charge of Attempted Murder in the Second Degree. Is that your understanding of what we are going to be doing here today?

THE DEFENDANT: Yes.

THE COURT: Have you talked this all over with your attorneys?

THE DEFENDANT: Yes, I have.

THE COURT: Has anybody threatened you or forced you into doing anything here today?

THE DEFENDANT: No, they haven't.

THE COURT: When you do enter this plea today, you waive, or you give up, the right to a jury trial and all of the rights that would go with it. If there was a trial, the DA's job is to prove you guilty beyond a reasonable doubt before you may be found guilty of any offense. If there was a trial, you certainly would have the right to get up here and testify at your own trial, although no one can force you to do that. You or your attorneys would also have the right to question anyone that testifies against you at the trial, and you would have the right to have witnesses come up here and testify for you. When you plead guilty here today, you give up all of those rights. Do you understand you are doing that?

THE DEFENDANT: Yes, I do.

THE COURT: Do you also understand when you plead guilty today, it is the same thing as if the DA proved you guilty beyond a reasonable doubt of this one amended charge, the same thing as if we had people here that sat here as a jury and listened to all the evidence, took a vote, and unanimously found you guilty of this amended charge? Do you understand it is the same thing?

THE DEFENDANT: Yes, I do.

THE COURT: Where did you go to college?

THE DEFENDANT: I went undergraduate to William Patterson College in Wayne,

New Jersey. My Master's Degree is from Syracuse University in Syracuse, New York.

THE COURT: So you certainly don't have any issues with the English language?

THE DEFENDANT: No, I don't.

THE COURT: Have you taken any kind of drugs or alcohol in the last hours?

THE DEFENDANT: No, just prescribed medications.

THE COURT: Does that prescribed medication affect your ability to understand what's going on around you?

THE DEFENDANT: Not at all.

THE COURT: Does it actually help you deal with what's going on around you?

THE DEFENDANT: Not those kind of medications, no.

THE COURT: What is it, if I might ask?

THE DEFENDANT: Neurontin, Celexa, vitamins, Ropinirole, and there is something else...I can't recall at the moment.

THE COURT: None of those medications or vitamins affect your ability to understand what's going on?

THE DEFENDANT: Not at all.

THE COURT: I will ask you, how do you plead to the amended Second-Degree charge of Attempted Murder?

THE DEFENDANT: Guilty.

THE COURT: Do you admit that on or about and during the month of October, here in Jefferson County, that you attempted to intentionally cause the death of another individual by entering into an agreement with some person other than the intended victim that would result in the killing of that victim in exchange for monetary payment? Do you admit those facts?

THE DEFENDANT: Yes, I do.

THE COURT: I have an appeal waiver in front of me now, Ms. Schonfield, and it does appear to have your signature on it. Actually, there is three copies of this. Did you sign all three copies of this?

THE DEFENDANT: Yes, I did.

THE COURT: Do you understand when you do that, you give up the right to appeal the conviction and the sentence that we have talked about here today?

THE DEFENDANT: Yes, I do.

THE COURT: People versus Melisa Schonfield on today for sentencing. The defendant agreed to enter a plea to the amended top count of the indictment and plead guilty to Attempted Murder Second Degree, pursuant to New York State Penal, which does provide for a wide sentence range.

The People agreed to leave the prison sentence and post-release supervision on to the discretion of the Court. The Court has indicated that the defendant will receive a sentence of five years state prison, followed by five years of post-release supervision.

This plea was further conditioned upon a forfeiture of the cash and cellphones utilized in an attempt to hire a hitman in this case. In addition to a crime victim fee and a ten-year permanent stay away Order of Protection will be issued in favor of the victim in this case. With that understanding, Your Honor, the People would move sentence at this time. Mr. Rossi, do you wish to be heard?

MR. ROSSI: If I may, Judge. Briefly. First, most respectfully, Your Honor, I have with me a copy of all of—as complete as possible of Miss Schonfield's medical record, which I believe would be of assistance to both her and to the Department of Corrections, and I would ask that this copy be made part of the Court's record and available to the Department of Corrections, if they don't receive it through our efforts.

THE COURT: All right.

MR. ROSSI: Thank you. Your Honor, as you know, a tragedy was averted in this case two times that I have noticed. One, when Detective Kittleson interrupted Ms. Schonfield's—Mrs. Schonfield's thoughts and concepts and put a cold stop to them. And second, when the Court gave us an opportunity to proffer everything that we had with respect to Miss Schonfield, and the Court gave recognition to the fact that Miss Schonfield's life and her character involved more than just the events of last October.

She struggles every day with serious medical and psychological problems. Despite that, she has been a terrific wife and mother and a good part of this community and a very successful professional in the healthcare area.

We are, again, grateful for the fact that the Court on the one hand has recognized the seriousness of this matter and that she must be punished.

But, on the other hand, recognized that punishment must be made in the terms of the totality of her life, and for that reason we are grateful, Judge.

THE COURT: Ms. Schonfield, do you wish to say anything personally before the Court passes sentence?

THE DEFENDANT: Yes, I do. Thank you. I stand before this Court today and I'm asking my family for forgiveness. My 82-year-old dad, my husband, my daughter, my son, and my friends but most of all, my grandson Eli, the little boy that I protected and tried to keep safe. I did this to myself, and now they're also going to be punished with my sentence. I'm remorseful of any and all embarrassment and humiliation that I may have caused to those who love and care about me. My only explanation is that I exercised extremely poor judgment out of fear when I believed that my grandson was going to be taken. As a result of that, I broke the law.

That not a moment goes by when I won't miss my family. Each day away will seem like a lifetime.

My past can't be changed, forgotten and/or erased, so I can only accept this punishment.

I'm grateful that the person in the car with me was a police officer. I would not have been able to move forward with my life knowing that I had something to do with taking the life of another being.

I would like to thank this Court for its leniency and for—actually for its consideration.

---

A Jefferson County woman who pleaded guilty to second-degree murder learns her fate. Melisa Schonfield, 57, was sentenced to five years in prison Wednesday, and five years post release supervision.

Schonfield, Melisa Rae SW: License 069999: NATURE OF COMPLAINT: The social worker admitted to the charge of having been convicted of Attempted Murder in the 2nd Degree. ACTION TAKEN: The New York Office of the Professions GRANTED the social worker's application for license SURRENDER.

# PART II: THE PRISON EXPERIENCE

There was a paper written by Harvard University sociologist Bruce Western on the role of prisons in perpetuating human vulnerability. I can tell you from first-hand experience, all of it is true. The following is excerpts from Western's paper.

The common narrative reserved for prisons and mass incarceration revolves around one word: retribution. American society, as a whole views prisons as places reserved for the most aggressive, dangerous, and malicious citizens whose actions are a product of some innate violent tendency. Prisons seem to reflect that—solitary confinement separates unstable people from their cohorts, beatings and abuse from officers mimic some crimes committed on the 'outside.'

In political debate about crime, it can be dehumanizing when people who go to prison are viewed as predators who prey upon the weak and innocent public. We didn't see that so much. We saw a lot of people who were struggling with a whole lot of physical and mental infirmity and a lot of other challenges in their lives. I hope a true accounting of human frailty in the prison population can help us think about mercy.

People are really struggling with serious mental and physical health problems, many of which had not been seriously or properly treated for a long time. People with mood disorders were also often struggling with chronic conditions and untreated addiction. There's a real physical and mental vulnerability in the prison population. It makes life after prison much more challenging.

We're often very focused on things like reducing recidivism and trying to produce behavioral change in people after incarceration to divert them from crime. But there are fundamental healthcare needs that people have.

We're really at a time where there's an opportunity to rethink the foundations of the system. Certainly, if we just think about the very specific problem of re-entry in the data I was collecting, there were three clear priorities: immediate income support, healthcare, and housing. If we zoom back a little bit and think about the system as a whole, we've imposed a very harsh punishment on people who themselves have been victimized— often over a lifetime—and people who are frail and vulnerable themselves.

This is the context in which we should understand how we respond to violence. "Our response of long prison sentences really oversimplifies a complex social reality that is just fraught with moral ambiguity."

# CHAPTER 6:
# RECEPTION AT BEDFORD HILLS

You either become bitter or you become better in here. I would have to make a proactive decision. A proactive decision that I would need to recommit to every day. It is not going to be easy.

Before I am transferred to the all-inclusive Taconic, the minimum/medium security prison, I spent eleven weeks in the maximum-security prison across the road: Bedford Hills. I am terrified. Many killers are here, lifers who will never be paroled. And then there was me. Initially, I did not make the connection that I am wearing green just like everyone else.

As I arrive and my leg shackles and handcuffs are removed, two Corrections Officers, known on the inside as COs, begin yelling as if we were in the military boot camp. As a group of the twenty-something of us newbies, we formed a single line to follow the CO to another building. This is DOCCS "reception." Reception? There is no welcoming committee walking around serving hors d'oeuvres and white wine. We are given a bag with an open nightgown, heavy bathrobe, a mini toothbrush and paste and Corcraft soap. Note the brand of soap. It makes white clothing whiter, removes the worst stains imaginable, and would cause my body to break out and itch.

We trudge up to the second floor. Hell cannot be this hot. The windows will not open more than a few inches, and most do not open it all. We are thirty-six women, many here on drug charges, violent charges, money crimes and weapons offenses. We will share three toilets, three sinks, two showers, a frightening-looking bathtub, and one floor fan. Apparently, the floor fan is a privilege, as is the cooler for ice.

We take turns in the basement speaking with the sergeant about personal safety, gang affiliations and scars, tattoos, and piercings. Dental records are updated, in case we ever need to be identified by them after our death. We did a Panorex to create a dental chart. The physician does a complete body cavity check. Nothing is off limits. They give us a written aptitude test and introduce us to our rehab counselor for the mental health assessment. It is rather amusing: "Do you feel anxious or depressed?" "Well, yeah. I'm in prison with notorious and violent criminals and I'm in the custody of people who really don't care about me but control me, so yeah, I find that anxiety-producing and depressing." "Would you say you are a danger to yourself or others?" "I guess the judicial system feels I am a danger to others, that's why they put me here." "Thoughts of suicide?" "Depends." "Any medications?" "Lyrica, Requip, Celexa, Mobic, Tramadol, Restasis, Zocor. I suffer from osteoarthritis. I have ocular myasthenia gravis. I was diagnosed with fibromyalgia on top of it. I have neuropathy from the three rods and fourteen screws after thirteen spinal surgeries. I have chronic pain."

# CHAPTER 7:
## LIMBO OR REALITY AT BEDFORD HILLS

Once classified, I am moved to the giant dorm that houses seventy-six women with only a three- quarter wall between them. I have the bottom bunk. I am being denied a medical mattress and my medications which NYDOCCS assured my attorneys and the judge I would be getting prior to my sentencing. The physician refuses to give me the medications I came to prison with. This is a problem, as side-effects from not being weaned can be unbearable, if not dangerous, but one thing you learn quickly in prison is that there is no case for the sane and rational, and you cannot argue on its behalf.

Bedford Hills Correctional Facility has been made famous by many inmates: convicted child murderer Lacey Spears, who killed her son with by overdosing him with table salt; Carolyn Warmus, who murdered her lover's wife; Judy Clark who was the driver for the Brinks robbery. Also housed there was Stacy Castor who sometimes was referred to as "The Black Widow." She poisoned her husband with antifreeze and then attempted to kill her daughter. Pam Smart was also there, serving a life sentence without the possibility of parole, for conspiring with her under aged student lover and other students to kill her husband. Now I was one of them. I wore the same green uniform, with the same corrections officers and we were all housed in the same facility—criminals, all of us.

The realization that there is no real difference between me and many of the women here was terrifying, depressing. The population of society I feared and looked down upon—I was now a part of. I was like Pam Smart, who was helpful to me as a new inmate. I was like Gigi Jordan, who killed her autistic son whom she believed was being abused by her ex-husband. She was pleasant as well. I sat with Mary Alice Tinney, who was convicted of poisoning her children and buried them. I was like her, too.

Still no medications and I suffer intense withdrawal. The rude and nasty medical staff had me spiraling into a hole I did not think I'd be able to climb out of. Finally, my husband at the time threatens NYSDOCCS. He says if I do not receive my medication by 3:00 the next day, he will not only sue, but he'll be contacting the media. I get my medications. But I paid the price for his insistence.

A few days later, the dorm is raided under the premise of searching for drugs. We are all removed from the dorm area. My cubicle is the last to be tossed, or rather inspected, and the one that receives extra scrutiny. I stand outside the doorway and watch. I observe my plastic hangers being broken intentionally. My water cup is smashed and dumped on the floor with my photos. My photos! They are stepped on. Photos are very precious in prison. The guards know that destroying a person's photos is irreparable, and cruel. The guards remove my mattress and toss it aggressively until it appears slashed. They throw my clothing all over the floor. It seems that sugar, which I do not own, is now all over the floor destroying what was left of my belongings, ruining the photos. I say, "Is this really necessary?" to the two female COs. "Shut the fuck up," they reply. I walk over to the two men in white shirts and say, "This is ridiculous, why are they singling me out?" He says, "Shut up or we'll take you to SHU."

SHU is an acronym for the Special Housing Unit. Solitary confinement. Another inmate pulls my arm to get me out of the dorm before the guards become violent.

I feel so violated. I feel raped again. I thought I dealt with that. It had been a long time ago—I was 15 when I was raped by a classmate in school. I told no one for a year and a half, until he attacked me again. Then I told a friend what happened. The next morning, my friend called my house as I left to walk to school and told my dad everything. My dad came to my school and together went to the police station. There, in a room filled with men, I would describe how I was raped. The embarrassment and humiliation ran deep.

This was a pivotal moment: I could either retreat inside myself or come out as a no-nonsense, fearless teenager. I chose the latter. I never let myself feel the fear. The court heard my case. My rapist was tried as a juvenile, not an adult, and so he never saw the inside of a prison. The judge sentenced him only to probation and a psychiatrist. Then the judge turned to me and said, "You should have trusted your parents." Really? Trust my parents? To what, to take care of me? My mother was on uppers Monday through Friday. Saturday, she slept it off and on Sunday, she was my mother for the day. Come Monday, the drugs would begin again. My father, brothers, and I all walked on eggshells. This was all another secret, but I never let it be a skeleton in my closet. A month later I learned that I was pregnant from that rape. Sixteen and pregnant. Abortion was not legal at that time. I found a "clinic" in New York City, in Chinatown, where, for $300, I would have an illegal abortion. That night after horrible cramps, I passed a thick blob of tissue, my rapist's baby.

The guards who ravaged my room have taken my few precious things and destroyed them, leaving a disaster for me to clean up. My peers agree: My bunk was hit the worst. Several women offer to help me put things back together and clean up. I decline. Instead, I sit on the metal frame of my bed with my arm over my mouth to muffle the sounds of my sobbing. The next morning, I clean up the mess, wash my clothes, and put things back in some resemblance of order. I assume the worst is over.

A couple of days later, I do what I always do at mealtime—I go for my Kosher plate. I am on the Kosher diet not because I keep Kosher but because the food is a bit better. We receive items such as oatmeal in packets, routine fresh fruit and vegetables, unlike the regular mess hall soy-based diet. Occasionally there is toast, sometimes cereal with milk, a can of tune or sardines, an onion—that would be my vegetable for the day. Dinner was pre-done, like a TV dinner, fairly disgusting but at least it came with an orange or banana. Since I am on the Kosher meal plan, I am permitted to pick my food up from the mess hall and bring it back to the dorm to eat. My dorm is empty. I lean over my bed to move when my bunkie, I assume, comes back from lunch. That is fine, I could use the company. But it is not my bunkie. Suddenly, an unfamiliar inmate slams my head twice into the top bunk, then once into the metal ladder going to the upper bunk, and leaves. Outside the doorway, I can see a man with a white shirt. Anyone ranking above CO wears a white shirt, such as a sergeant, captain, lieutenant or deputy. He is watching. I lose some teeth, there is a lump above my right eye, my head is bleeding.

I know that the rules require me to report every cut and bruise, otherwise there is a punishment. Yes, you get punished if you get injured and choose not to report it. So, I have no choice. I walk myself to medical and fill out an accident report. I write, "I hit my head on the metal frame of the upper bunk." I am not lying. I dare not say how or who made my head hit the metal frame of the upper bunk. If I did say that who knows what the next round of retaliation might look like? Who knows what else could happen to me? I was afraid of dying in prison.

Soon after the assault, I am told I am moving across the street to Taconic Correctional Facility, as planned. Thank God. I never thought I would be excited to go to a new prison. I hear it is a lot better, a less restrictive environment than Bedford Hills. I have a short time to assemble what is left of my things. I get four white burlap-like bags called draft bags. Everything I own is itemized before I can pack. There are issues. I have too many personal shirts, so the COs throw them out. I do not believe for a minute my new personal shirts would remain in the garbage can for long. I have a bit of food which is open and therefore cannot come with me. I am stripped and searched and then handcuffed with a waist shackle. I board a transportation bus and go literally across the street to Taconic.

# Chapter 8: Life at Taconic Correctional Facility in Bedford Hills, New York

Taconic is a small facility housing roughly 300 women. It is less than 500 feet from my door to the outside yard. There is a recreation room with two phones and one TV. There are four small buildings with cells, a tiny medical clinic, a mess hall, a school with a storehouse and commissary in the basement. I am assigned a single cell to myself on the first floor, and luckily the package and visiting rooms are within fifty feet. Things are looking up. But not for long.

Three days later they move me to "The Shelter." No, I don't know why I am moved. Nobody is obliged to explain reasons in prison. "The Shelter" is altogether different than my initial Taconic accommodations. Imagine fifteen beds and fifteen lockers all in one large room, with no privacy whatsoever. The bathrooms are down the hall. The showers are tiny, disgusting, most without curtains or tiles, reeking of mold.

After two weeks in "The Shelter," I am moved yet again. No I do not know why, and I now know better than to ask. I'm moved to a two-person, very cramped room. It is deafeningly loud, and the women are anything but calm. I witness an older woman start a physical fight with another inmate. She gets sent to Lock, which is different than SHU. In Taconic, if you are in Lock, you get put in separate gallery for 23 hours. One hour is for recreation. The gallery where Lock is located is in the same building as the lobby and visiting rooms, and it is very restrictive. Twenty-three or twenty-four hours a day are devoted to being locked in the cell, which has heavy metal bars, with an opening through which your food is passed. Showers are allowed every other day, phone use is restricted to one ten-minute call per week, and the only way to be social is to yell out the window in the hopes that someone from other nearby galleries feel like talking.

Later that day another inmate, dubbed Beyoncé, takes to dancing wearing only state- issued granny panties. She used to prostitute herself for drug money and she was also a stripper. Her breasts keep us laughing as they almost hit her in the face. I had forgotten how good it feels to laugh. Beyoncé comes over to my bed and sits down. Clearly, she had been a meth addict. Her teeth, rather her lack of teeth, her shuffled walk, tell the story. She wants candy and knows I have some. She starts massaging my feet. I had also forgotten how good feels to be touched by another human being. I relax a bit. Then she starts moving up the calves of my legs. When she gets to my knees, I stop her. I figured out her intentions and put an end to it. Beyoncé will become an ongoing problem in our unit and shortly thereafter, her incessant inappropriate behavior lands her back in Bedford Hills, the maximum-security facility I pray I will never have to see again.

## Shower and Poop, Oh My!

Several days after moving from the shelter into the temporary two-person cell, I go to take a shower. The setup is archaic and filthy. A normal-sized body must carefully move into the stall so as not to touch the walls. Alone, I remove my robe, turn the water on, step into the shower to find a pile of human feces, a full load, on the drain. I put my robe back on and call the CO we refer to a "Ratchet-W." I ask her to step into the shower room and show her the drain. She puts her shirt up over her nose and says, "Clean it up." I stated very clearly, "No, it's not mine. I didn't do it." "Clean it up." Then almost pleading I said, "I can't, I have medical restrictions, no bending, lifting, mopping, sweeping, shoveling." "Clean it up." "I physically can't do this." "Clean. It. Up."

I know what is next. If I do not clean it up, I will be sent to "Lock" for disobeying a direct order. Of course, it makes no sense, but in prison, nothing does. So, am I to stand on principles or just clean it? I triple glove myself and get to work. It is almost impossible not to vomit. Finally, when I leave the shower room, the CO says, in her condescending voice, "I'm not saying you did it. I am not saying you didn't. I just said to clean it up."

## The Rules of Medication

Two to four times a day, depending on our needs, we wait on the medication line. This is an event unto itself. With the paperwork and privacy laws now enacted, (HIPAA), one would assume the rules also apply to DOCCS. They do not. We all know each other's ailments and medications. There is no privacy of any kind, even the ones guaranteed by law.

I go for medication twice a day, once in the morning when chow has been called and again at night, which translates into anytime between 7:00 and 8:30 P.M. It is like fighting a pack of wolves, these med lines. Literally the moment chow is called the entire facility shows up for medication and waits. Rain, shine, sleet, snow. Inmates wait on a line so long that we are standing outside without any shelter. I am unsure how anyone could think this is effective.

There are a few crucial lessons to learn on the med line. Check your medications before ingesting. You never know what you might accidentally get, as prescriptions are sometimes distributed carelessly, and you may swallow something you should not. I for one, do not want anyone else's HIV medications, male hormone medications for transitioning, Hep C medications, or psychotropic cocktails. All I want is the Lyrica and Prozac I have been prescribed. Next, I learn that "cheeking" one's medications and then selling them for cigarettes seems to be a popular way to take care of one's nicotine addiction. I watch women drop their medications into a scarf around their necks, cough into their hand, or just stash the pill somewhere in their mouths. Sadly, if caught or even suspected, the officers and sergeant will detain you, handcuff you, and haul you off to Lock while you wait for a hearing on the charge. That will not be me. I really need my medications, which I've yet to realize will become a constant struggle while in prison—even when released from prison, as nobody cares about a prisoner's or a felon's medical needs.

**Groundhog Days…Same Shit, Different Day**

Incarceration is an endless experience in loneliness. Here in Taconic, the only thing consistent is the daily inconsistencies in this broken system. One can be rebellious, or one can become institutionalized. It is a daily struggle. Every morning I open a Corcraft state-issued sanitary napkin and turn it into a Swiffer. I clean the greenish-black residue from my windowsills, the screen and floor. I have a tiny sink in my room with only cold running water. I also have a toilet. Taconic is one of the few facilities where inmates get single cells/rooms. The bare necessities are taken care of. I multi-task in the shower—I bring my laundry with me, as we are not allowed to use the sinks to wash out clothes. So, I bring a shower caddy and a blue bucket filled with laundry soap and the day's uniform. For my sheets, towels, and personal robe and blanket, I pay someone in the State Shop a pack of Newport cigarettes, or some commissary, for the weekly laundry assistance.

Cells must be incompliance by 8 A.M. This translates to one plastic chair cleared of any clutter, the bed made military-style, and nothing but a bible outside the locker. Everything else needs to be well hidden, not only from COs but also from other inmates.

## 15G0717: My Identity

No one really cares about who I am in here. No one attends to me as long as I can breathe and have a pulse. This is becoming a familiar experience. No one in the whole system cared about me all along—surely not the police officers who failed to protect my daughter and grandson, the detectives who took advantage of my naivete, the judge who legally could not consider the circumstances leading to my crime and sentence me to mental health care instead. Not even my lawyer, who never told me I actually had the right to an appeal—that I had 30 days to reverse my waiver even after I had signed it. The moment I signed away my rights, he dropped me as a client and disappeared.

I have no identity except a DIN. A DIN is assigned to each inmate admitted to the Department of Corrections and Community Supervision. This is an internal number used as an identifier for the inmate while he or she is in the custody of the Department. The DIN has three parts; a two digit number, a letter, and a four digit number that together reveal the year of an inmate's initial admission, her DOCCS reception center, and a sequentially assigned number within the reception center. Even the medical clinic is not interested in my name.

## RIOT, the Real Inmates of Taconic

This prison is not a safe facility. The building is full of asbestos. In the event of a fire, one CO would have to manually unlock between 36 to 72 cells. Inmates in Lock never get to participate in a fire drill. It is impossible to manually open all the cells quickly.

The personalities here with me span the spectrum and some inmates jail much better than others. Most friendships are superficial at best. But these are my friends. We refer ourselves as RIOT, the Real Inmates of Taconic, and we all do the same thing at the same time in the same way.

6:00 A.M. is the first Count. This means overhead light on and sit up or stand. I am usually up and dressed by then. I like to get up at 5:30 and do my push-ups, squats, and stretches while it is still quiet. I think

I also get up then because the mess hall workers leave at 5:30 to go to work and they are noisy. By 6:45 Count is "cleared," and our doors are unlocked manually one-by-one. The kitchen door is unlocked, and we are permitted, with restrictions, to prepare our own food. There are two hotplates (four cooking burners, assuming they are all functioning which is rarely the case). But cooking may not begin until 8:00 A.M. Depending on the CO, we are permitted to put our archaic metal coffee pots on the hot plate in the kitchen at this time.

7:00 A.M., before we are permitted to make breakfast, we are allowed to use the phones. Access begins at 7:00, two pay phones per unit. I call my brother and Alexis and Eli. At 7:20 they call chow and medication for general population. No one is permitted to carry certain classes of medications. The opioid epidemic is outrageous in here. I have been offered and have also declined big bucks for my Lyrica. 8:00 A.M. marks the beginning of programs and recreation. One can go to the very limited gym, or to one's service program. Since I am one of the few prisoners with a master's degree, my program is in the school building. I am an IPA, Inmate Program Assistant, for a pre-HSE class. Nevertheless, my abilities are underused, as I have been reduced to grading papers, keeping student records up-to-date and paper ripping. Yes, I said paper ripping.

11:00 A.M., back to the unit for Count. 11:45 to noon, Count is cleared. I do not understand why it takes so long to count 300 women. Noon-ish is Chow. I only go to the "zero-star Michelin rated mess hall" when there is pizza. Pizza is by far the DOCCS' best meal, though still part frozen and worse than elementary school cardboard. 1:00 P.M., programs and recreation begin again. I am medically unassigned in the afternoon, which means I either help women with their math and reading, or I knit or read, and often fall asleep for an hour or so. I do not go to the yard for recreation. I have been to the yard three times since I arrived. It is risky. The yard is where too much happens, and I do not want to be a part of it. 3:45, everyone returns for the 4:00 P.M. Count. After about 4:45, the phones become mayhem, and since we all argue over phone entitlement, inmates have been reduced to phone lists. 5:00 P.M. Chow. I cook with "the cartel." It is a barter system; I give them food and they cook one really good meal a day that we all share. It is a means of survival, as there are no fresh fruits or vegetables available on the commissary or in the mess hall. But, each inmate is allowed to receive thirty-five pounds of food per month from the outside, sent to them in no more than two monthly parcels. That may sound like a lot, but when you consider how heavy fresh food can be, it is actually very little. But thank God for it. 6:00 P.M. is the third programming activity. Monday nights there is yoga. Tuesday and Thursday night offers parenting classes. I did a little bit of facilitating. Wednesday night is knitting. Friday, there is occasionally Bingo. Saturday and Sunday the facility broadcasts a movie on Netflix. The director of recreation selected "interesting" movies that none of us were usually interested in. There are religious services once a week for different affiliations. 7:00 P.M. is medication at the clinic again. 9:45 P.M., everyone goes back to their unit for the 10:00 P.M. Count and lock in. Every day is the same. I am incredibly alone.

## Loving Family Equals Punishment...Again

I should have recognized the signs for impending doom. The school building had the day off, some sort of training holiday. This was supposed to be an unassumingly easy Friday. I reluctantly agreed to help another inmate fix the baby squares she was assembling for a family visit the next day. She was frustrated and I was not happy at how she sewed it, so I took it apart and reassembled it for her. I had everything out on the table in the rec room. Instead of listening to music videos or hip-hop, I claimed ownership of the remote and I put a movie on the television.

I was in my happy place when the CO bellowed my name. "Yes!" I responded. All she said was, "Trailer now!" I thought I knew why. I have been trying to prepare for an interstate transfer to be near my dad's house in Santa Fe, New Mexico. I have been holding on to notarized paperwork from him for my counselor. So, I assumed I was being called for that. I threw on my shoes, grabbed my cane and the papers, signed out and went across the walkway to the trailer. I was blindsided.

A DOCCS investigator, not my counselor, had requested my presence. She had a few issues to discuss with me. "It has come to my attention that your brother has called the Clemency Board in Albany on your behalf many times," she said. It was true, he had been fighting for clemency for me, based on my medical issues and overall ill health. "Yes, I believe he has." "Your brother is harassing people in official roles," she went on. "That's not his intent," I whimpered. "I will interview your brother, at which point he will be charged with a crime and banned from visiting you." I tried not to cry but I was shocked. How could this be? She delved into my history and my brother's legal history. I told her my brother was stressed living in Florida and trying to make a living while caring for and visiting my dad in New Mexico and me in New York State DOCCS. She asked for his phone number and I obliged. Three times she tried calling and the line was busy. Impossible. He has a cellphone, with call-waiting and voicemail. I left the trailer quite shaken up and promised to speak with my brother.

Fortunately, when I arrived back on my unit the telephone was available. I called him, hysterical. As calmly as he could, he squelched my tears and assured me this was nothing to worry about. New York State DOCCS does not like it when family members get involved with the forces in power, and they were just trying to rattle me.

He seemed to be right. While the investigator assured me my brother would be contacted, he never was. The three calls she made to him while I sat there were a ruse. Four days later, someone actually contacted him, and the situation as explained was not at all similar to the magnitude of my interrogation. Sadly, this is a subtle retaliation for my family doing nothing more than demanding something better than sub-clinical and sub-therapeutic medical care for me. But NYSDOCCS is still in the draconian days, only more socially acceptable, and punishments are less obvious. No one on the outside really understands this, and I will bet very few of them would care. After all, the attitude of most civilians remains that inmates are nothing more than society's garbage.

My brother had also called the facility on several occasions trying to make sure inmates could receive ice daily in the summer heat. It did not go over well, when he inquired if they had lost the recipe to make ice.

Clearly, I led a very sheltered life. I knew this population existed, but I never thought they would be housed in one place, with me. Prior to this adventure I didn't care about this population. That has completely changed.

## Ineffective Communication...Intentional?

In 2015, New York's Governor, Andrew Cuomo, announced the creation of an Executive Clemency Bureau to identify people in the state's prison system who might be worthy of commutation. The announcement sparked hope among the system's approximately 50,000 prisoners, their families and advocates that they might soon rejoin their families.

Clemencies can take two forms. There is a commutation, or the shortening of a person's prison sentence, which allows an incarcerated person an earlier parole hearing or an immediate release. The other form is a pardon, which expunges a person's criminal conviction altogether (which governors have used to prevent people from being deported). Governors have the power to issue an unlimited number of clemencies.

What does "being worthy of commutation" entail? According to Cuomo's criteria, an applicant must prove that he or she "has made exceptional strides in self-development and improvement; has made responsible use of available rehabilitative programs; has addressed identified treatment needs; and the commutation is in the interest of justice, consistent with public safety and the rehabilitation of the applicant." Cuomo's criteria also require that a person has been sentenced to at least one year in prison, that they had already served at least half of their sentence and are not scheduled to appear before the parole board within the next year.

Cuomo encouraged attorneys and law firms to donate pro-bono hours to help incarcerated people prepare their petitions. Many heeded the call and devoted significant time and resources to helping dozens of people imprisoned across the state. But these efforts have not proved fruitful. While word of Cuomo's commutations initiative spread quickly in some mens' prisons, many incarcerated in womens' prisons were unaware of it.

"We're in direct contact with people inside the womens' prisons," I had heard, though reports revealed that three-quarters of those women had not heard of the governor's clemency initiative. The news reported that "Valerie Seeley, the only adult domestic violence survivor among the governor's 12 commutations, has confirmed that between 2015 and her release in January 2017, she had seen no posters or announcements about the clemency project. More recently, 61-year-old Melisa Schonfield, who is serving a five-year sentence after attempting to hire an undercover officer to shoot her daughter's abusive ex-boyfriend, only learned about the governor's project—and the possibility of pro-bono assistance—after her family paid a private attorney to help with her clemency petition. Schonfield, whose health has been declining while in prison, told her daughter that there were no announcements about the governor's project in the prison's common areas or even in the law library, where she recently spent many hours working on her application."

## Clemency Letter

Dear Clemency Board:

My name is Melisa Schonfield. I am writing on my own behalf. I am a first-time offender. Unfortunately, my crime is of a violent nature: 2nd degree attempted murder. While I did accept the minimum plea, the punishment is still severe in its duration. Had my crimes not been made high profile by the media, and my family's position in the community so well-respected, perhaps the

D.A. would have been more amicable to a lesser charge with different consequences. I am not a vigilante, although my crime does appear that way. I gave up fighting with the Family Court system and committed a crime. I believe my hyper-vigilance trying to keep sane while protecting my daughter and grandson from a man I perceived as an abusive bully would have been served better in a psychiatric unit and not a dangerous prison environment. Reactive behavior rarely ends well. I can contest to that! I was a law-abiding, community-serving member of society prior to my crime. I suppose even the best of us fall sometimes. I made one huge mistake and it cost me everything. I am going to be 61 years old in January. I have served half my sentence. I have endured more than most at my age. My body is riddled with osteoarthritis. I suffer with fibromyalgia. I suppose I should have thought about the domino effect prior to committing a crime, but I was not in my right mind. I make no excuse for my actions. I am remorseful. I am aware that clemency is rarely if ever awarded to someone like me. I still believe in justice and the penal system to do the right thing. I am able and ready to take care of myself again. I just need you to afford me the opportunity.

Respectfully submitted, Melisa Schonfield 15GO717

**More from RIOT**

I have what feels like sorority sisters in here and I care about them. We all have a story. Theirs count just as much as my own. First there is my neighbor across the hall. She thinks everything is "lit" and twerks well enough to dance back-up for Miley Cyrus. The problem is, she is also illiterate. She kept this a secret. For a while she had me writing for her under the pretense that she did not have spellcheck abilities in prison, but it became clear to me that she could not read at all. I find it incredible, in this very day and age, to barely be able to read and not write or do math.

This woman was enrolled in ART, which is known as Aggression Replacement Training. She had assignments, so I would write her homework as she dictated it to me. I tried to help her. I would replace "He do" with "He does," and other basic grammar. But I cannot save her from herself. She is so loud. She has no inside voice. She is either twerking and yelling or sitting in the rec room listening to music videos or hip-hop. Another young inmate held her brother while he died—they were shot. She lived but has a significant brain injury. Regardless she was the most obnoxious and disruptive woman on the unit.

Then there is the poster inmate for what a sociopath looks like. This one thinks she is pretty and petite. Her story was on *Dateline*. She tried to hire a car salesman to kill her fiancé's wife. How can, one have a fiancé' if he is still very much married? She insisted that she was set up, but the audio and video cameras captured it all. She was the mastermind. When it aired, she gathered us in the rec room to watch her debut. She was smiling and pleased with how she looked, and I was embarrassed for her. She insists my crime and hers are identical. I have not figured out how. I tried to hire someone to hurt/rid my grandson's abusive father. My only goal was to keep my family safe from an abusive bully. But she was motivated by greed. This inmate's self-image is one of generosity, kindness and honesty. She is anything but that. She plays a good victim. Her line every day is, "This can't be real," to which the answer from me is, "Pinch yourself. It's real."

I met a woman who became a real friend, when she came to this unit. I found her crying on the phone. My friend is well educated, no drug history and very humble. She was convicted of a financial crime and very embarrassed by it. She takes medication twice a day like me, so we have become "The Twins." I am five foot two and she's five foot ten. We joked that she was Arnold Schwarzenegger and I was Danny DeVito in the movie *Twins*. This friend was like a daughter and a peer all in the same breath. We understood each other's hearts and mourned all we had lost by coming to prison. We learned each other's moods and could call each other out. When I had thumb joint surgery and was in a cast for six weeks, it was this friend who helped me shower, zip my coat, do my laundry and dishes. I taught her to knit and she helped put love back in my heart.

The two Spanish women, a.k.a. the cartel, are the gentlest and most nurturing women. Yes, despite both having murder convictions. When my friend received an interstate transfer to Arizona and left Taconic, they began to cook for me. I gave them most of the food that I get sent in from my brother: fresh veggies, cheese, meats, and they did all the cooking. They always checked in to make sure I am okay. I feel guilty for my lack of participation in all the prep and clean-up tasks, but it works for me and them. Spanish was the only language they could speak before coming to prison. Now they speak English.

There is a race war of sorts going on in this facility. I was rather appalled at how some COs refer to inmates based on skin tone. I was considered light skinned by some of the "dark-skinned COs." The dark-skinned COs tend to let behavior slide with other dark-skinned inmates. It is just what happens here, and we all know it.

My prison family and I grew closer, but I should have known to keep my guard up. I was very fond of one Haitian woman. She is in for murdering her husband. What I believed was genuine and caring was only grooming me for the next crime. She had cooked for me, taught me better knitting skills, and we confided everything to each other. But she was beyond manipulative. For example, if I let any inmate look at my new knitting magazine before her, she did not speak to me for over a week. She was a prolific knitter. One day she asked me if an inmate who owes her $800 for what she had knitted could send the money to my brother and then he could send it to her. I asked her why not send it to her new husband? She replied she did not want him to know. I did not feel comfortable asking my brother to do this as he is already overwhelmed caring for our dad and me. She did not make a fuss as she normally would have with her vows of silence. I thought nothing of it.

This inmate was removed from our unit for bullying and fighting with many other inmates. The last straw was calling an old-timer, soon to be released, "Crack head." The superintendent got involved and yet she acted like she was untouchable, but guess what? She is not. She still wears green. Several days later I realized she moved housing units—along with my five jars of face cream, scans of yarn, and all my food. Here is the connection: I was helping my illiterate neighbor figure out her monthly inmate financial statement. There were two withdrawals, each for $90, that she insisted she did not make. I had her request copies of her signed money disbursement from inmate accounts. Not only was it not it her signature, but the CO's signature was also forged. So much for my so-called friend, as she was actually the forging culprit.

As I digress, many of the inmates here have addictions in addition to their crimes. I wish I could say the prison alcohol and substance abuse treatment, ASAT, is effective but, frankly, it is a waste of resources. Addicts will do anything to get what they want. I learned to never do cigarette business with an addict, as I have to look at the daily package list and run downstairs under the pretense that I'm on the list, when the only reason to be there was someone who owed me cigarettes got a package. It is a shame to have to track people down who owe you something.

Frankly, why is tobacco use even permitted in prison? Outdoors it is like a giant nicotine cloud. I feel like I am a smoker with all the second-hand smoke. I used cigarettes as many inmates do as a monetary means with purchase power.

Back to my so-called friend.... After an investigation she was charged and put into Lock. She got 45 days. Anything over 30 days means the offender will go to Bedford Hills CF and serve time in SHU, special housing unit, a.k.a. solitary confinement. But she was never transferred and served less that the time she should have. Why? A certain LT got involved. Like this inmate, she's dark skinned, and, like this inmate, in-house she's always polite. The old-timers inform the rest of us that she did the same thing when she was in Bedford Hills CF some years ago. Part of the scam was to drag me into it. My brother and I would have been charged with money laundering. Wow! I am naïve. She was no friend. She never apologized to me. Instead she looks the other way when we run into each other in the walkway.

## Long Shot

Watertown Daily Times Newspaper Article – March 2018

The daughter of the woman who was convicted of trying to hire a hitman says her mom should be let out of prison. Back in 2014, Melisa Schonfield tried to have the father of her daughter's baby killed. Schonfield eventually pleaded guilty to second-degree attempted murder.

Now, her daughter Alexis is petitioning for her mother's early release due to several medical-related issues that are going untreated at Taconic Correctional Facility.

"She has hardware in her back, she's had several spinal surgeries, artificial knee; I believe she has Myasthenia Gravis [a chronic autoimmune neuromuscular disease that causes severe weakness in the skeletal muscles, which are responsible for breathing and moving parts of the body, including the arms and legs. In most cases, the first noticeable symptom is weakness of the eye muscles. In others, difficulty swallowing and slurred speech may be the first signs. The degree of muscle weakness involved in Myasthenia Gravis varies greatly among individuals, ranging from a localized form limited to eye muscles (ocular myasthenia), to a severe or generalized form in which many muscles— sometimes including those that control breathing—are affected].

"There are a lot of other conditions as a result of those issues," Miss Schonfield said.

An attorney claims Melisa isn't receiving the proper care she requires. And Alexis told the Times she is afraid her mother will "come out beaten, and almost feeling defeated and lost." There is also an online petition to show support for Melisa Schonfield's release.

Melisa Schonfield, 61, was represented by Syracuse attorney Emil M. Rossi during her 2015 trial. Renee M. Wong from Goldberger & Dubin, P.C., New York City, is now representing her in an attempt to have the sentence commuted.

Ms. Wong said Mrs. Schonfield's history of nonviolence prior to her conviction should also be taken into consideration for her early release.

"In addition to her medications, there are things she needs like orthopedic shoes and compression socks that are so basic to people who aren't incarcerated," said Ms. Wong, "that can take up to two years to be delivered in the Department of Corrections system."

According to the state Department of Corrections and Community Supervision website, her earliest release date is in November 2019.

Ms. Schonfield and Ms. Wong said Melisa's medical condition is also an issue they are highlighting in the commutation case.

"I know it's prison, not summer camp," Alexis Schonfield said, "but I'm afraid she'll come out beaten, and almost feeling defeated and lost. There's a difference between a medical accommodation and a comfort." She said that her mother was not a violent person; "if she saw even a fly die, she would practically want a funeral for it."

She said her mother's decision "still doesn't make much sense to me ... But I don't think it was meant to be malicious or cruel. I just think we do things out of fear, maybe." She described her relationship with Mr. NAME REDACTED as abusive.

"It's hard for Department of Corrections facilities to provide the level of care she needs," Ms. Wong said, "and her staying in a state facility creates a burden on taxpayers."

The executive commutation lawyer, Ms. Wong, is working toward is an "extraordinary release," which can be granted at the governor's discretion.

"The odds are against us, but we won't stop trying to free Mrs. Schonfield. There are so many people in the community who care about her," Ms. Wong said.

Mrs. Schonfield spends her time in Taconic knitting and creating children's books for her grandson. Alexis said her mother sends one to him about once a month.

Along with letters attesting to Mrs. Schonfield's character, an online petition was also created to show the community support for her early release.

## Reflection: January 30, 2016

My husband ambushes me, telling me, not asking me, "We're getting a divorce." I remember pleading, begging, "Please don't divorce me, I need you." I was sobbing. He said, "No." He had already begun the paperwork. I am flooded with fear and despair. At that time, life without my husband was unimaginable, unfathomable. After thirty-seven years of marriage, and after five years of incarceration, I was to be single again. My thoughts were spinning uncontrollably, and there was nothing I could do from the inside of these barbed wires. What will my life look like? Where would I live? How could he leave me? How could I breathe without him? What happened to 'til death do us part?

I am destroyed. I barely recognize myself. What happened to that happy, confident woman I used to be? Where did I disappear to? What about the price I am paying for the act we both participated in? Where did I go? I used to be able to speak to anyone about anything and everything, and slowly I retreated inside of myself. I used to be excited for life and fun to be around, and then I became a "ball and chain." Nothing would frighten me, and now I find everything is terrifying. Especially being alone. And a future alone, life on the outside, my release, alone—just the thought was crippling.

After that, my husband saw me once more and then never visited again. For a long time, I kept hoping he would show up to tell me that he loved me, and we would work it all out. I played the scene, over again in mind. But of course, that did not happen. I never got any more letters from him, or time with him. All I received were receipts of funds that he had deposited into my commissary account monthly. I was frozen in myself and in time.

My husband, meanwhile, had completely moved on. Plans were already underway to sell our house. I suppose I was an idiot to be so surprised. The perfect marriage I thought I had was not so perfect, really. I knew that my husband had a series of extramarital affairs, many of which I discovered on my own, others I had heard about. Our marriage had been deteriorating for some time.

My husband and I began as polar opposites. He was introverted, often thought of as arrogant, but at the same time he was a firm decision maker. On the other hand, I was an extrovert. I could talk to anybody, no problem, and I shot from the hip. I tried to pinpoint when he began to feel so differently about me, and I think it began when we had our first child, our daughter Alexis. I was too tired for my husband, but his dental assistant was not.

Most of our friends were my friends. I chose well enough that my husband was able to enjoy the company of their husbands. Years ago, we grabbed a burger at a sit-down restaurant at the mall. I remember having my husband look at the couple by the wall, and telling him, "I never wanted that to be us. They just ate. They did not talk, except to their waiter. Person-to-person, they didn't talk...." I did not talk, and then, over time, we became that couple, and we would eat in silence. My husband was obnoxiously polite, but not a word passed between us. I thought we were strangers just eating at the same time. Then I began to loathe going out to eat. He even began flirting with waitresses. I felt invisible.

Sex became infrequent. It lacked any kind of excitement, but that is just not what I missed the most. I wanted to see the warmth in my husband's milk chocolate eyes. I wanted to feel wanted. Anything, just look at me, talk to me, hold me. Our conversations became routine, talking only about our kids, grandson, work. Our lives became so mundane. Once the emptiness arrived, I became unsure of my role in life. We stopped being a team, so we crumbled. Our life was a blurry routine, no room for passion.

I am sure other people would consider our marriage fairly, ordinary. My husband provided for our family financially, and I took care of raising our family and caring for our home. This was all in between my thirteen spinal surgeries. I believed I would always love him and be waiting for him. Ironically, I would never see him as my husband again after the day he told me we would divorce. He had taken off his wedding band several months earlier, the gold band frayed. He had it repaired and never wore it on his left ring finger again.

In spite of this, I was in total denial the day he left me in the prison's visiting room. I still loved my husband. We were supposed to grow old together. I was supposed to die just one day before him, so I would never know the pain of a life without him. I actually believed he would realize how ridiculous it was to even consider a divorce and apologize, but that never happened. It did not have to be this way. I would have forgiven him like I always did.

And now I felt dead. The feelings of despair left me completely spent. The pain was unbearable. I could not eat. All I did was cry and sleep. I felt like someone sucked all the air out of the room. And I kept thinking... maybe I had pushed my husband into seeking attention from other women. How could he just throw me away? Why was freedom from me so important? Was it his own guilt? I yearned for what I lost every time I looked at the pictures. It was my family. We looked happy. Was it a lie or was it someone else's life? I thought constantly about our thirty-seven years as husband and wife as if it were a movie. I tried to understand my part in what had happened. I walked around depressed, and even my body began to feel the depression. I made myself alone in the loneliness, it was overwhelming. There were no antidepressants that could help this time.

Everyone in Taconic could see my immeasurable agony from my husband's visit, and my anxiety grew as I tried to imagine my future without him. That agony plagued me for two years. Then slowly, there was one day when I did not cry, and then there was another. And I reflected on the key events in my life.

I have been through a lot in my life. My mother was a drug addict and alcoholic. I came to realize this when I was only 12 years old. It was 1969 and the first time I was aware of my mother's drug problem. My dad found her overdosing and drowning in the bath tub. My dad had to have her committed to the community psychiatric hospital. My mother's drug and alcohol events escalated in 1978, when my dad was dealing with cancer in his knee. He came home from a stay at Memorial Sloan Kettering and was in a weakened state. But my mother was using drugs and alcohol to the point where she could no longer function. She threw a wooden ice chest at my dad. It missed him, and I ducked out of the collision course. This time I was the one who had my mother committed to a psychiatric hospital, to the Carrier Clinic. She was there for a month.

It was difficult going to family meetings there. I hated them. I did not like Al-Anon. I did not care about anyone else's story, as nothing could take away the pain or give me back my mother. When she was discharged, I made sure to have lunch with her every day. It was almost a year before our relationship was on solid ground again. My dad still met me Tuesday nights for dinner, unbeknownst to my mother. He always made sure I was okay.

November that same year, over Thanksgiving weekend, I had my first date with my future husband. By the end of December, we were living together and engaged. We married in 1980, in Westbury, New York, honeymooned in Saint Maarten, then moved to Fort Knox, where he was stationed in the Army.

Meanwhile, and for the next two years, I was undergoing a series of spinal surgeries— more than five—and then a miscarriage. But in April 1983, Alexis was born.

Several years later, while getting my hair cut, I listened to several military wives talking about their dentist. The blood drained from my face as I heard my last name, and how this dentist was offering to trade sex for no dental bill. This could not be happening to me. Me? Never! I had a great husband, didn't I? I lived in denial, craving and choreographing the "perfect life" with the "perfect husband," and I convinced myself that both were true.

Why, you ask? Why would a smart, educated woman with a career as a social worker blind herself to the truth of a bad marriage to an unfaithful man? Why did his approval mean everything to me, and why did I love him through his double life, his lack of kindness, his lies? I am not a victim, but I blamed myself for everything that had gone wrong. I was not available enough... I put my career first... my repeated surgeries left me sore and unattractive...I was a mother first, a therapist second, a wife third. Whatever story I told myself, I believed it. I am codependent. After every indiscretion of his, I would get a piece of jewelry or a trip. I had my first cruise to Venice and Greece, the most intimate of travels, but he would not touch me. Why? Who was he faithful to if not me?

I am sure on some level, I knew there was nothing I could do to make my husband change, but I never stopped hoping he would remain faithful to me. What did this mean for me? Watching the eyes of my husband focus everywhere on everyone except me. Making love and knowing he was not with me, rather looking out the window, and imagining he was somewhere other than in the present. He quit kissing me. Sure I would get a peck on the cheek every now and then, hello or goodbye, but the interest, the passion, was gone. Yet I always had hope. I would have to make a change. I would have to decide whether I wanted to continue to put up with his double life. I never had the guts to form a list of consequences and stick by them. Instead, I just hurt and became distant. Was this an addiction?

I took our vows in 1980 seriously: "...in sickness and in health, for better or for worse, 'til death do us part." Could I justify ending this marriage, the family we created, our history, companionship, all of it? We had been through too much, and I thought the trauma would be the one reason to hope this man would be the husband I mistakenly thought I married. I know I am codependent, and I did in fact marry some version of my mother. But I never wanted a divorce. I still believed in my husband. I did love this man, or the man that he had been, yet I am all alone.

**Never underestimate your memory.**

In 2005, we built our McMansion, as they say. The ideal house on the ideal street, to contain the "ideal family" people thought we were, that

I convinced myself we would be. I told myself this house, these gifts, our future were all fueled by love, but in hindsight, his gifts were out of guilt. In the end, my husband would not give me the one thing I asked for: his heart.

Money buys distractions, and we had plenty of them. My husband would purchase things only to have them, but never to use them. I bought a tiny sailboat. He would not go out with me. We bought kayaks. He paddled out once. There were golf clubs, hot tubs, clothing sprees, vehicles, etc. Nothing penetrated my misery, in fact he plugged the misery with spending even more money on things we did not need.

I guess I was mistaken when I assumed my expectation of marriage was universal. I expected to marry a man who was loyal to me as I was to him. I loved that he was loyal until I learned that he was not. My husband would act exhausted all the time, he started putting his phone in his pocket during all waking hours. When he received a text, he would come alive. My foolishness came from believing him that the texts were from our son. They were not. I should have left him. What did we ultimately have in common? The big house? Grandchildren? Grown children? What would he take from me if I left him first? Would he care or would he be relieved? I should have paid more attention to the reviews from his patients because they reflected not only his skills as a dentist but, ultimately, his character as a human being.

All of us, whether we reside inside or outside the gates, need healing. We all build our personal prisons and commit ourselves to sentences there. Even though we have the ability to release ourselves, many of us never do. But now, incarcerated at Taconic for many years, prison is just geography for me.

I am free from my ex-husband. I do not think I could have recovered like this if I had not been in prison. Because in prison, I found me. I had the support of some incredible woman who had been through similar experiences, and a few COs who were good to me. People would not let me be alone; everyone made sure I was all right. I thought I could not breathe without that other half of me. And when The Fourth of July came, which would have been my anniversary, I sobbed. But in the year that followed, I realized I had been in an unhealthy marriage, and I wondered why I stayed. I understood that I deserved the respect he never gave to me.

And then, with that shift inside, I looked back at my life a bit differently. I did not realize my depression had set in not just after our marriage ended, but during it. My self-confidence was traded down for self-doubt and anxiety. I do not think I realized what a lie I was living. Coming to prison awakened me to the fact I was living in a prison long before I got here. I realized that before all of this happened, when I was "free," I had lost any ability to free myself from the prison of my mind.

There is no actual rehabilitation in prison. That is a fallacy. There is a lot of time for self-reflection, lots of dwelling, the potential rehabilitation of ourselves. Sometimes prison is a gift. Prison helped me get myself back and not seek anyone else's approval. I guess when I came to prison, I learned how to stop hating myself. But at the same time, as odd as this sounds, I came to believe that I am where I am supposed to be right now. In prison I finally lost the 250 pounds that my husband weighed on me. Prison allowed me to take the time to heal. I spent too many years doing it all. Only prison afforded me the opportunity to hang that Wonder Woman costume in the back of my closet. My adult timeout has given me something I am not sure I could have found anywhere else. I am not useless or unlovable. I am imprisoned, and I will heal myself.

# Part III: The Light at the End of the Tunnel

## Farewell Letter

Ms. Schonfield,

Honorable is always the first word that comes to mind when I think of the type of woman you are. Driven is the second, and compassionate is third. Why, in that order? Who knows? To know you with and without your story has defined honorable to me. Having been through your situation despite landing in this place makes me feel as though I wish I had a mom like you. Not that my mom is a bad person, but you always say what you mean and mean what you say. You can be very direct, which is sometimes difficult for people to hear, but you are always delivering the message of a life lesson in a very compassionate way. Your determination and drive everyday requires an extreme amount of strength that a lot of us lack. It gives me hope for myself and the courage to face my demons, and to know that no matter the outcome, there's a lesson learned and it does not have to define the person that you are. Meeting you and the RIOT Sorority, has truly been a rare blessing in my life. Selfishly, I will be very sad without you here. But I also know it's your time and chance to live your life to the fullest, not to focus on anyone else but yourself and find what makes you happy. Congratulations on your LCTA. I will cherish these next couple of months with you.

Love, Your Coffee Buddy

## People Do Not Always Take Advantage of Those in Green...

I have my hopes set on LCTA—Limited Credit Time Allowance. This is for violent crimes in addition to merit for good behavior. By working as an inmate program assistant (IPA), or completing and passing 24 college credits, an inmate can earn the subjective privilege of having six months reduced from her sentence. In my case, my LCTA, coupled with time for good behavior, could get me released 8 1/2 months early. I was all in. But there was a catch. Because I came in with a master's degree, there was no education opportunities for me to pursue. The problem is that I was medically unassigned. This left me working two years as an inmate program assistant, an IPA. I asked repeatedly since arriving in Taconic in November 2015, for the IPA training, a two-week class. But no classes were formed until November 2016.

I worked for more than two years as a teacher's aide as well as one summer school for another teacher. The class was ridiculous. To work as an IPA all you needed was a GED and no behavior tickets, and at least one year left on your bid. I am a licensed social worker. The lessons were ridiculous. This is prison, I have no opinion anyone is interested in hearing. Upon completion, I interviewed for a teacher's aide position in the school building. Ironically, the principal would not employ me due to my medical trips, yet she approached me to work with the teacher no one wanted to work with. The teacher that no one lasted with interviewed with me for 10 minutes and asked me to work with her.

The principal wanted me to work two program periods. I only agreed to one. "I'm coming out of retirement for this?" I also struck a deal with her that if for any reason after one month I did not want to work with this teacher, I could switch teachers. She said, "90 days," and I repeated myself. Reluctantly, she agreed. It bothered the principal that I was also the rabbi's clerk and unknown to many, she was part of my tribe. It is all in this unspoken language. So, for $.246 an hour, which is not even 75 cents for the morning, I was to work from 8 until 11 A.M., Monday through Friday. My job began as something mindless, taking attendance, handing out books and erasing pencil marks in all the workbooks. I would also like to make the point that these books are not new. While the information may not have changed, publishers do update books. Prison budgets are so pitifully small that for inmates, keeping a small, carbon footprint makes it manageable.

On day three, I found myself making drawings on scrap paper before falling asleep. The teacher did not allow me to help in any other way until day seven. She made a huge deal about a project she needed done and wanted me to complete. She took three pieces of paper, folded them in half lengthwise. I got it so far, then, using a pencil, she pressed the crease and tore the paper. "Okay, and?" And that was it. She gave me a pile of paper and reminded me, "Only three pieces of paper at a time." "Screw that." I took a chance and grabbed four pieces, then seven, then with over confidence, ripped less-than-perfect paper. She cringed, and stopped writing on the board to come over to my table. She was angry that I did not follow her three-paper rule. She said that my tears were not even. She took the paper away from me. I failed paper ripping.

Hey, I am a craftsperson and I have a graduate school degree, so I was never asked to rip paper again. It felt like one of my own kids who did a horrible job not washing the floor, and then was never asked to do that chore again. Hey, I am catching on to this prison thing and jailing better. One day the same teacher I worked for let me write the vocabulary words on the board. Students put them in alphabetical order before writing definitions. So as not to put anything in order, I scattered the words on the blackboard. She didn't like this technique either. I was not asked to do it again.

There is a theme here. I am not a quitter by nature. So, I chose to stick it out. I can tolerate most situations. I found myself no longer feeling guilty about my numerous medical trips off the compound. This teacher became tolerable. However, her racism still made my stomach turn. Her teaching her own opinion about abortion, and addiction, and psychiatric disorders irked me. I started to discreetly correct her. Sometimes I really believed she detested inmates and looked at us as her charitable, do-gooder project for herself. Summer came and there was only one instructor teaching. Summer school was three and a half weeks of class with an air conditioner, not so bad. As OCD as the main year teacher was, the summer teacher needed organizational skills. I could overlook that as students thrived in her classroom.

There was no class in August and no summer school. The following summer of 2018, the Deputy of Programs stated if there was no school through no fault of my own, the time not worked would still count. December 4, 2018, was my two-year commitment to the end date. I went to apply for my LCTA and was denied the privilege. Albany said I owed four months.

The Deputy was wrong. One must apply six months prior to a release day on an LCTA. So now I was told I could not even apply until March 2019. That meant I could not leave until September. I would miss my son's and his fiancé's two weddings (a traditional Chinese wedding in December, and an American wedding in June), Eli's seventh birthday, and my ailing dad. I was a mess. I was called down to see the

Deputy's replacement. I needed my "shake and wake" repaired. It is an alarm clock for the hearing-impaired. Mine broke. While I was there, I took a chance and mentioned the situation with my LCTA.

The stars must have been aligned, as this was part of her previous job. She seemed sincere and said that she would recalculate my time owed and do her best to push my LCTA through and still get me out May 23, 2019. On Friday afternoon, my ORC, called me to her office. I am grateful to both she and the Deputy. I got my LCTA and I am going home, wherever that may be, on May 23, 2019. I kept my poker face when I was told. My prison kin found out when I was going home, and I cried. And then I smiled, and we hugged.

I am going home. It is almost over. It is not real, I am scared, nothing is the same. I have no home, no marriage, a family divided, no professional license, an ailing dad.

Could it be the weather, no. It is beginning to rain so why does my knee still hurt a little less? I had slept remarkably well Friday night and did not care that I had no master schedule for the week ahead. I called my brother and said, "I won't be needing new sneakers. I can buy them myself. I'm coming home." He was so supportive, firm, but gentle with me. "Enjoy the moment, and there will be many more," he said. I called both of my kids and told them I needed a big favor. "Please buy me blue sneakers, size eight." Both refused, reminding me blue is a forbidden prison shoe color. I retorted. "Not if I wear them on the 23rd of May 2019." I am coming home. It is over. I am tougher, stronger, and still tender. But mostly, I am freer than I ever have been. It is only geography, this prison.

My son asked, "So Mom, what song do you want to dance to at my wedding?" "I can't even believe that I'll be at your wedding!"

Eli and I had been counting the days since I came in here. About a year ago, I made him a calendar of each day, noting how many days left. I told him I am coming home, and he just wants to make lasagna and cookies with me. All I want is for him to take my hand as I leave the gate.

## 1,330 Down and 55 to Go

March 29, 2019, day 1,330 of 1,385. 55 to go. The weather is changing, I can feel it in my knee. I can see the gate from my cell window. Soon I will walk through it. I am always so happy when I see women go through. I watch and I smile. I enjoy seeing their parole clothing. It is not a green uniform, rather it is clothing sent to them from home usually. Then after they cross the gate, I turn around and cry. I do not see myself walking out the gate. I never believed my time would really come. I could not see it. Now I can. There is an end to my *Dante's Inferno*. The ending feels as surreal as the crime I did in the first place. It is like a movie on the big screen, only it really is my life.

Prior to this adventure, I thought felons and ex-felons, there was no difference. I could not and would not associate with someone who had been incarcerated. Now, I am the thing I loathed, only I no longer loathe any part of me. I committed a crime but that does not make me a criminal. I paid a severe price for a bad judgment call. I trusted my spouse and that trust was betrayed on many levels. Could I date an ex-felon? I do not know. And who is going to date this ex-felon?

## 52 Days and a Wake-up

Fifty-two days and a wake-up and I am out of here.

The only constant here is the inconsistencies. Today we were called for morning medication. Halfway there, we were told that medications are not ready. Go back. How difficult is it to have medications ready at the same time each day?

I went to school and spoke with the new Education Director. Since I have met my two-year-plus IPA obligation, I want to retire. I will need the time. I have so many medical trips coming up and a possible surgery for my nose.

My brother sent me 16 of the 35 pounds of food I can receive. I waited on the package room line for half an hour with another inmate. She came to help me carry my bags since I have a medical limitation. No lifting over 10 pounds. No sweeping, no mopping, no shoveling. Whatever. They inspected my packages. I was not aware that this pizza sauce is no longer permitted. But, according to this CO, this month I cannot have it (interesting because the pervious month, I was permitted the pizza sauce). Instead of arguing, I signed a disposal form for it to be donated to the women's shelter, but not before a "sergeant review." I went back upstairs, only to be called back down. The same CO I had just left, told me I was" being slick," writing sergeant review on my sauce rejection. Then he proceeded to tell me that the sauce is not and never has been permitted. That is funny because for over three years, I have been receiving this identical product every month.

I am used to nothing making any sense at all. I have been waiting since 2017 for reimbursement for an electric razor that was denied but was waiting for my family to pick up on a visit the following week. I had my hairdryer taken by a CO in a room search, though I had a permit for it. My DIN was not engraved on the hairdryer. The CO said that she would send it down to the package room and I could pick it up the next day. My hairdryer vanished. I had cigarettes taken out of my packages. Friends told me that they sent six packs, and somehow, I only received four. Trying to succeed and collect on a claim is comical. Somehow it gets turned around, and the inmate is blamed for the missing items. "Casket-Ready" suggested I was lying about two sets of knitting needles that I was not permitted to receive. We call her "casket-ready" because she has worn the same hairpiece, as long as I've been in Taconic, and enough makeup for cadaver viewing. She asked who the CO was that made the denial call. I did not remember. Her comment was ridiculous. "Well, I would remember if someone would not let me have my things." I gave her a name, but I was wrong. The Sergeant checked and that CO did not work that day. Okay, I am sorry, but my knitting needles are still unaccounted for. To date, I have not been reimbursed for any of the items lost and/or missing. I hope whichever CO took it needed it and enjoys it.

## Philip Zimbardo's Stanford University Experiment

Philip Zimbardo's Stanford University Experiment could, still, be cited for its accuracy when it comes to the dangers from misuse of power in a prison. It is probably one of the most famous studies of our generation. I studied it in school. In 1971, psychologist Philip Zimbardo set out to create an experiment that looked at the impact of becoming a prisoner or prison guard. The researchers wanted to know how the participants would react when placed in a simulated prison environment.

## He had said:

Suppose you had only people who were normally healthy, psychologically and physically, and they knew they would be going into a prison-like environment and that some of their civil rights would be sacrificed. Would those good people, put in that bad, evil place—would their goodness triumph?

The researchers set up a mock prison in the basement of Stanford University's psychology building and then selected 24 undergraduate students to play the roles of both prisoners and guards. The participants were chosen from a larger group of 70 volunteers because they had no criminal background, lacked psychological issues, and had no significant medical conditions. The volunteers agreed to participate during a one to two-week period in exchange for $15 a day.

The simulated prison included three six-by-nine-foot prison cells. Each cell held three prisoners and included three cots. Other rooms across from the cells were utilized for the jail guards and warden. One tiny space was designated as the solitary confinement room, and yet another small room served as the prison yard. The 24 volunteers were then randomly assigned to either the prisoner group or the guard group. Prisoners were to remain in the mock prison 24 hours a day during the study. Guards were assigned to work in three-man teams for eight-hour shifts. After each shift, guards were to return to their homes until their next shift. Researchers were able to observe the behavior of the prisoners and guards using hidden cameras and microphones.

And the results were horrifying. Originally slated to last 14 days, it had to be stopped after six due to what was happening to the student participants—the "guards" started to abuse them, behaving in ways that were aggressive toward the prisoners, while the prisoners became passive and depressed. Five of the prisoners began to experience severe negative emotions, including crying and acute anxiety, and had to be released from the study even earlier. And then it got worse. The researchers themselves began to lose sight of the reality of the situation. Zimbardo, who acted as the prison warden, overlooked the abusive behavior of the jail guards until graduate student voiced objections to the conditions in the simulated prison and the morality of continuing the experiment.

Only a few people were able to resist the situational temptations to yield to power and dominance while maintaining some semblance of morality and decency; obviously, I was not among that noble class.

Zimbardo later wrote in his book *The Lucifer Effect:*

So, here's what this experiment tell us: It demonstrates the powerful role that the situation can play in human behavior. Because the guards were placed in a position of power, they began to behave in ways they would not usually act in their everyday lives or other situations. The prisoners, placed in a situation where they had no real control, became passive and depressed. And that is what prison is really like. Power and passivity. We all play our roles.

For example, last night's CO literally tore apart one room, to the point where he flooded her floor and she had to retrieve the mop and the pail. He dumped the bucket with ice that stored our commissary chicken and cheese. It was not called for. The directive reads, "For room searches a CO is supposed to return things either back to where they found them or neatly on the bed." I suppose keeping everything contained in the room they searched qualifies.

It has never made any sense to me how I can be medically restricted to my room and yet climb stairs and walk to the clinic every day for medications. No one understands how if you are locked in as a punishment, medications are brought to you, but if you are a medically restricted inmate, you are punished by having to walk and get your medications at the clinic.

At least we will not get blood clots—oh, wait a minute, I had at least one documented blood clot. When the outside temperature reaches 70 degrees, they put the heat on. Why? Oh, why does not really matter. I think this is a passive-aggressive punishment, as it only serves to make us hot and miserable. And if inmates are not miserable, then COs are not doing their job. To be fair there were a few that I will never forget who treated me with dignity and respect. They were not passive aggressive and were not intimated by my intellect and worldly experiences.

## More from the RIOT

The end to this nightmare is coming, and I am waking up.

April 2nd, 2019. Tuesday. It is 5:00 A.M. Why am I up? My neighbor, of course. She felt the need to announce in her loud, raspy, inside voice, "Goodbye, goodbye, goodbye." as she was being released today. Just go. It is 5:00 A.M. Since I am wide awake, I may as well start my day. Every morning, I do leg exercises and stretching before getting out of my bed. Then I do 50 or more pushups. I do not get excited. I cheat since I do them on a slant. I continue with 50 squats and 50 arm lifts using my bed for equipment.

My window faces the gate to freedom. Guess who is now under my window, getting her handcuffs and leg irons to go across the street to go to Bedford Hills Correctional Facility? Yup, the "twerker" is there. Shortly, they will bus out. She is still on her farewell tour. Just go already. Finally, someone yells, "Shut the fuck up!" Oh, how you read my mind.

Then someone opens my door, as if to trying to sleep is nothing more than an exercise in futility. I have no work today or tomorrow as students are testing, so there is nothing for me to do. My Mexican friend asks if I want a jam and mac and cheese. Jam? Why would I want jam? She laughs and repeats "jam" again. The third round, she describes the jam. She is making yams. I just love the accents. I feel like I hunt for translations. Last week, she asked me for my calculator. I took apart my locker and had located it for her. She did not understand why I was giving her a calculator. Lost in translation, she needed to borrow my coffee pot. Calculator, coffee pot. Sure, they sound alike.

My other Spanish friend is even funnier. Apparently, my unit thinks I am a full-service bodega. I guess it is good because I usually have whatever someone needs. I do not like asking for things, so I make sure that I have as much as possible without hoarding. Anyway, she asks me for a "cooley." Okay. What she is really saying? We have a back-and-forth for a while before I realize it is her "cooley." She has hemorrhoids and needed pads. Yeah, I have them. Tucks are multipurpose in prison because they are soaked with witch hazel. They make for a great face toner too. Since we are not permitted alcohol, they can clean tweezers and nail clippers in a pinch.

The room across from mine is barely aired out when I see someone else moving her things in. DOCCS only allows inmates to house in a room for one year. Her one year was up so she moved two doors down with all her worldly goods. She is Muslim and has taught me a lot about religion. As a Jew, I am astonished by the basic similarities. What is more incredible, in this horrific setting, a Jewish woman and a Muslim woman can not only get along but have each other's backs. She helped me navigate the trials and extreme tribulations of a divorce I neither initiated nor wanted. We both have hearing-impaired signs on our doors. When her hearing aids died, I gave her a spare pair to use.

She is also a student at Bard College. I get to read, correct and edit many of her papers. I enjoy it. It gives me back a few lost IQ points.

Today, several women I have tutored are taking their exams to either move up in class or take their GED. I took a lot of time helping them, ripping apart their essays and teaching them how to read multiple-choice tests. I hope they pass.

### *One Day You Will*, **Lady Antebellum**

*You feel like you're falling backwards, like you're slipping through the cracks,*

*Like no one would even notice if you left this town and never came back.*

*You walk outside and all you can see is rain.*

*You look inside and all you can feels pain, but you can't see it now.*

*But down the road the sun is shining*

*And every cloud there's a silver lining*

*Just keep holding on*

*Every heartache makes you stronger*

*It won't be much longer!*

*You'll find love*

*You'll find peace*

*And the you you're meant to be.*

*I know right now that's not the way you feel, but one day you will*

*Wake up every morning and ask yourself, what am I doing here anyway?*

*With the weight of all those tears and disappointment whispering in your ear*

*You're just barely hanging by a thread*

*You want to scream but you're down to your last breath*

*But you don't know if yet.*

*But down the road the sun is shining*

*And every cloud there's a silver lining*

*Just keep holding on*

*Every heartache makes you stronger*

*It won't be much longer!*

*You'll find love*

*You'll find peace*
*And the you you're meant to be.*
*I know right now that's not the way you feel, but one day you will*
*Find the strength to rise above you will*
*Find just what you're made of, you're made of*
*But down the road the sun is shining*
*And every cloud there's a silver lining*
*Just keep holding on*
*Every heartache makes you stronger*
*It won't be much longer!*
*You'll find love*
*You'll find peace*
*And the you you're meant to be.*
*I know right now that's not the way you feel, but one day you will*
*I know right now that's not the way you feel, but one day you will*

## April 11, 2019

It is 3:14 A.M. I love the quiet, before even the birds wake. I would enjoy the night even more if I can just manage my pain enough to sleep. To the left of my bed, as I lay here, there is an area where we are permitted to hang things. I call it my wall of shame. I have photos from most of my visits over these incarcerated years. My now ex-husband with Alexis, Eli and me on a bench in the Bedford's Correctional Facility. There is Thanksgiving with the entire family and my dad, my brother, friends, and relatives, too. My favorite thing is a drawing Eli did where he wrote, "Home is the Heart," and he is correct. Home is not your address or where your stuff is hung up, home is where your heart is. One of the very few things I will not leave behind is my photos. I have had more than 100 visits.

I am taken to my next medical visit. I have a replacement knee, three rods and 14 screws in my spine, not to mention metal in my hand joints, but I am in the van and I am handcuffed and shackled. Where, exactly, do they think I am going to go? Not to mention any escape intentions cost seven added years to the Five-Star New York State Department of Corrections amenities. This includes a cot, hot water, free clothing allowance, 24/7 surveillance and all the electricity and hot water you want. Believe me, I would rather be stranded on an island with two-year-old quadruplets.

A new inmate moved into the unit; I could not help but hear her phone conversation. We have two pay phones, but some inmates are loud. She is professing her love to her husband, while attempting phone sex. Lovely. I need to remember to germicide the phone and chair before I use it and bring a tube sock as a receiver holder. No sooner did she hang up then she went to the rec room and had her hands all over her girlfriend. Women in many of these lesbian relationships forget about their girlfriends when their family comes to visit on the weekend. Many are married to men. Some women enter the lesbian world after being betrayed by men. Nevertheless, on weekend visits from the family and friends, their girlfriends are all but forgotten. I do not judge her. The loneliness can be mind-altering. We do what we must do to survive.

## April 20, 2019

Today, I am legally divorced for two years, it seems like another lifetime. I do miss the marriage when it was healthy... when it was happy and working for us. I miss having an exclusive relationship.

One inmate left here about six weeks ago, after 27 years. She had pneumonia. Aside from sub-clinical and sub-therapeutic medical care in prison, there is no plan to make this ex-felon healthy again. My plan is to see a doctor for a real physical, sometime in June, and get my vitamins and medications right again. I have been deprived of so much over the last, almost, four years and, now I am paying the price with physical problems and pain from the neglect.

It is not that hard to keep inmates healthy. But no effort is made. NYSDOCCS chooses the cheapest foods and the cheapest medical. We are all ill in some form or another, often many ailments. There is so little fiber in our diets that we all need to take the polycarbophil pills to avoid constipation and hemorrhoids. Without fiber pills, constipation and hemorrhoids are like a contagious disease. Prison foods give inmates diabetes. The boots and sneakers create bunions—the podiatrist is a regular visitor on the compound. Hearing aids are plentiful. Acid reflux is a chronic problem, probably diet-induced as well. Arthritis seems to be a general term along with IBS and eczema. If hydrocortisone, Benadryl, or hemorrhoid cream cannot fix it, an inmate is screwed. Case in point, my hand surgery took three years to happen, my nose seven months and my knee injury, from Labor Day 2018, was finally addressed as needing surgery from a tear only this past week. M-R-S-A, Methicillin-Resistant Staphylococcus Aureus (MRSA), is a bacterium that causes infections in different parts of the body. It is tougher to treat than most strains of staphylococcus aureus—or staph—because it is resistant to some commonly used antibiotics. It is easily contracted in here, though M-R-S-A is not as easily contracted in the world outside these walls.

The mold in the facility is not only dangerous, but unconscionable. Rodents are in the buildings. Asbestos was never removed. We have all been exposed during the year-long window replacement project. Our hair falls out easily, our skin is creped and dry, teeth become brittle and there are no root canals or periodontal work. The tooth is just extracted.

One of the reasons inmates are so unhealthy is because we lose the motivation to fight the system for humane treatment. Obviously, humane is a subjective term. Furthermore, I think some inmates refuse to have medical care because they are fed up with the unreasonable control bestowed upon them and refusing treatment gives them control.

Ironically, medical refusals need to be signed at least 24 hours prior to the medical trip, otherwise, you are going to the appointment. Inmates are not supposed to be made aware of outside trips as it is considered a "security risk." One will wear handcuffs, waist and leg shackles in the van to the medical trip and wear those same accessories on the way back. I suppose we do not have a choice here, unfortunately, there is no third option in favor of what an inmate wants to do.

Everything outside has turned green overnight. Taconic no longer looks like a back alley waiting for a limo with a machine gun to pull up. It is a bleak place without foliage.

I have concluded that NYSDOCCS is humiliating, as well as tortuous. If we stop in front of someone's door, it is a cross-visiting ticket as soon as any part of the inmate crosses the threshold. It is a Tier III ticket, going into any cell, other than your own. The punishment is, "Lock" for 30 days, loss of commissary and, basically, LOL, not laughing out loud, but called "Loss of Life."

The punishment is coming to the prison and, certainly, that is more than enough humiliation, but the sneaky underhanded ways some COs, sergeants and lieutenants try to find an inmate doing something wrong, it becomes torture. The rules do not apply to everyone.

At Taconic there are some serious racial issues, there are serious control issues and then, of course, there is just some simple-minded people in an easy position of power, abusing inmates under the auspices of Custody, Care and Control. I have always said, "I'm in their custody, they have control over me where I have none, and they truly don't care."

## Pain Means I Am Alive…

Another miserable night. I tried to make a hoist for my left knee, but it did not work out so well. I should not have used my velour blanket. Between my knee and my hand, my body must be in inflammation overload and, of course, it is allergy season, too and the air quality is poor.

Being here made me realize my deep fear of the blue or gray uniform I have had since I was raped. I have come to realize I feared the wrong thing. It occurred to me early this morning, I fear the abuse of power when someone puts on the uniform. And that growth is a sign of emotional health.

It is Earth Day and I finally got the surgery for my nose. I am "healing."

## Cruella de Vil and Inept

Cruella de Vil, the CO, had company last night, and the laughter and the high intensity of sound coming from the rec room woke me at 1:48 A.M. If I hear her yell "puppies" I will run! I suppose the torture of denying me sleep continues. I am feeling better, though. I put my tablet radio on, stuck in my earbuds, and at least zoned out until mess hall workers were roused at 4:30. It would be so much easier to be pleasant at the job you choose to work at than it would be to be a miserable, spiteful CO.

The unit's young inmate is all wound up this morning, and all I asked was to turn the news on and not watch music videos. Then her mouth began to run away with itself, and the volume made it extremely easy for the entire unit to have to deal with her disturbance. One of the easygoing COs is here today, and for him to lose his cool, this unit must be awful. We were also informed "casket-ready" Sergeant is putting our housing unit under a microscope. Cameras and microphones are being watched live. It is like being arrested all over again. What is the real crime here? An inmate stops in the hallway to say something to another inmate? Being social is a part of being human, but then DOCCS does not think of us as human beings. We were only a commodity in a warehouse that clearly is easily replaceable. Big Brother is real here.

"Inept," as I prefer to call this mean and nasty CO, was in the clinic this morning. I really hoped she would have said something to me about last night. She was angry, and threw the clinic door open, pushing past me and just missing injuring me. Her attitude of entitlement is a familiar inmate personality disorder, only she is a CO.

I left the rec room to avoid listening to the up-and-coming young inmate's outbursts. I am fine in this room called a cell.

This is day eight since surgery. My bruising is now in the yellow to green stage. Yellow is just not my color! It turned into a cool rainy afternoon. I went into the rec room, and they were all watching *Black Klansman*. I heard it is a good movie. After half an hour, I could no longer tolerate all the racial slurs. As we had all decided to change the channel. I said, "Wait, Spike Lee is making his point by being so offensive." We kept it on. Ironic, isn't it, with the color war going on in here in prison, what a movie to watch. I am hoping after watching this movie some of these women will stop calling each other "fucking this" and "nigger that," and realize how it sounds, and the impact that the language has around any of us.

The Lieutenant walked by my room while I was talking to my neighbor. She looked at me and asked what happened to my nose. She thought I was in a van accident on an outside trip. This was the most she has spoken to me since I arrived here in November 2015.

It is raining so I put on my clear, full-length—and I mean to my ankles—raincoat and hood. It is so humid I began to sweat, and it launched a full allergic reaction to the post-surgical adhesive tapes. Prison has taught me how little I really need to get by. I hopped into a cold shower, put a cold compress on my head after I dressed, and did something I used to instruct patients suffering from traumas: tapping (also known as EFT, people tap on certain parts of their body to relieve anxiety and PTSD), and it worked. The distraction really made my body calm down.

No one gave the "oldest inmate" on this compound what she was asking for, so before Count, an ambulance came for her. Chest pains. She is a 76-year-old inmate. She was not seeking attention. She was trying to get medical care. I hope it is not her heart, and it is just the stressors of the Taconic Correctional Facility. We may never find out.

## April 23, 2019

No word on how the old inmate is doing. Last I heard, she was smiling and talking as she was put into the ambulance.

It is a little after 2:00 A.M., and Cruella de Vil was entertaining again. Why are they so loud when 36 women are trying to sleep? No answer is necessary here.

My welts had been frantically itching and my face is swollen up with hives, while the remaining tape is flapping like wings in the wind. The actual splint is still intact. I am beginning to think as civilians we unnecessarily burden the healthcare system, asking for so much treatment and care. Here I am 62 years old. For the last four years, I have had a limited and sub-clinical and sub-therapeutic medical attention, and yet here I stand.

It figures I fell back asleep at 4:01, only to be woken by my door unlocking and a flashlight. Field trip. I hope the splints in my nose come out today. I will find out where I am going shortly. Our evening CO was not our usual officer. I swear, he looked like he was in traffic control with the flashlight. We went to Westchester Medical Center. My splints were removed. Have you ever considered what it would feel like to have your nails pulled out from your nostrils? Me neither, until this morning. Two-inch tubes looking like clear pea pods were pulled out, and then five stitches between my nostrils were removed. I must wear the outside splint for another week, and then I will see the surgeon next week.

My nose looks great. The left side of my lip no longer droops. The rash from the adhesive tape is not attractive by anyone's standards, so I am in bed on this gorgeous day while I air out my face.

Done in DOCCS's best ineffective format, the Eucerin cream and nasal spray I left at the infirmary a week ago was handed to me on the medication line tonight. Fortunately, I had extra of both; if I did not, my recovery might have been delayed or impaired. I could have walked in leg shackles there and back in under two hours. Why did it take them seven days? The CO would not allow me back into the room to collect the medication after I had been strip searched. She would not give it to the Taconic COs who were picking me up from the infirmary.

In my absence this morning, the Sergeant had "The Sociopath" moved from our unit and relocated to the building furthest away. She walked around as if she got what she wanted, a smug look on her face.

Have you ever noticed a disturbingly long nose hair, or perhaps just was made aware of it because it tickles? Well, I thought it was a hair, but then when I went to pull it out, I learned that it was a stitch that was firmly, attached to the inside of my nose. We are not permitted scissors, so the old-fashioned toenail clipper becomes the MacGyver go-to tool. I could not fit it in my nose. I tried holding it, or a tweezer, and then cutting it, and that wouldn't work either, so I rolled it in the tweezer and gently relocated in its position to a more stable place in my nose. I have a raw butterfly rash with blisters from something as gentle as paper tape. Perhaps if the clinic would have done any kind of follow-up, this could have been avoided.

My assigned parole officer is going to meet Alexis and Eli Friday night. Things are starting to move forward. My release is near.

**April 24, 2019**

**1,356 out of 1,385. 29 days to go.**

It's "wacky" Wednesday. It's a training day for Taconic employees.

After morning medications, the Sergeant gave the mess-hall worker a problem as she tried to deliver my Passover holiday meal. Apparently, the hierarchy here believes only Jewish people can touch kosher food. I never knew that, nor do I believe it. Even if it were true, I am medically restricted to my unit, and my meals are delivered to my room. Furthermore, the food is in Styrofoam to-go boxes. Anyone could deliver it. Not a holiday has gone by where the feeling of discrimination, segregation and humiliation have not shown at least one of their discerning faces.

What a gorgeous day. The sun is out with a gentle breeze and the humidity is low. The foliage is blooming, and the green and yellow coloring remind me that I am not dead. Life is around me. Survival in prison is not just about staying alive.

This sounds shallow, but I stayed with the Jewish community not because of my religious beliefs—although I have enjoyed my time with the rabbi and the Tribe—I've stayed because of the food. On the holidays, we receive fresh fruit and healthy salads.

I question my relationship with God. Yet I remain strong. Maybe food is the way to believing in God. I will go with that. Then there is my "higher power." I give thanks for the fresh and healthy meals, unlike the soy-based, nutritionally deficient foods that NYSDOCCS serves in the mess-hall.

Alexis met up with my parole officer. She is allowing me to go to my son's wedding at the end of June. I am feeling overwhelmed with thoughts that I still have no control over my own life. Parole is not freedom and I do not know how it really works. Is my parole officer a poor travel agent or an overzealous babysitter? Either way one slip and I am back I prison. I paid my price to society with 1,385 days of my life. I feel like post-supervision is just a double or triple jeopardy.

Things are so quiet without "The Sociopath" starting trouble or chasing others for affection. The east side has three empty rooms, and four of us are medically restricted to our cells with feed up trays. Our housing unit looks like a hospital ward now. On the west side, Taconic's "oldest inmate" has not returned yet.

I am getting anxious about my dad's health, and my inability to get to him now in New Mexico and afterwards because of post-release supervision. Apparently, he and I are living parallel lives. In one way or another, we've both been frozen in the ninth ring of Dante's Inferno. My brother is stuck in the middle, going crazy trying to take care of us, all the while seeking a reliable income.

### April 25, 2019, Day 1,357 out of 1,385

Three more Thursdays and I am out the gate. I do not know how but I slept straight through from 10:00 P.M. count to 6:00 A.M. Count. While I am not tired, my face is so swollen, clearly, I did not sleep elevated last night.

My neighbor still was not brought back after her arterial procedure Tuesday, the plan was to return yesterday. Yesterday, she was brought back to the doctor. Apparently, she was put in the infirmary. I hope she will be back today. Seriously, the east side is having a lot of health issues. For both of their sakes, I hope the two women in the infirmary from my housing unit are not roommates. The fighting would end very badly for both of them.

I think the anxiety I'm feeling, the racing to go to nowhere, stems from my fear of seeing firsthand how easy a parole officer can violate a parolee and send a person on post-supervision back for the duration of her sentence. I do not see myself wandering extremely far from my humble abode with my daughter and grandson.

My nose feels like I am wearing binoculars with assistants holding them in place. I am miserable.

One CO that liked me stopped and asked me if the "old lady" was being bullied by "The Sociopath." I said she did what sociopaths do. He said her eyes are vacant and told me she was moved to the housing unit by the yard. She had better watch it over there, she will be taught a lesson in the showers. There's so much less tension since she left our unit.

I took a two-hour morning nap with my tablet under my pillow and my earbuds. Prisoners get tablets now, but without any connection to the outside world. I listen to music daily now. Prior to incarceration I was a music afficionado. I punished myself by denying the sounds I adored.

Someone gave me four *National Enquirers*. Somehow, I always have an abundance of books and various magazines in my room. Mail call. I have none. How is that possible? I think the mail person of the day decides to distribute one piece of mail per inmate per day and then shreds the rest. I am missing magazines and weekly letters Alexis was told by friends of mine, they are in the mail. At least I am not getting any bills yet.

It was suggested that our housing unit be a little gentler on ourselves. We have too many medical trips, surgeries, and overnight stays, which takes up the COs' time, so there will be no outdoor rec. While this does not affect me, because I do not go to the yard, it is a punishment for the other inmates. The only way one can socialize with another inmate from another unit is in the yard, or if you have a common job or location. My personal belief: The yard is where so many problems develop, pill-passing, note-passing, affection, sex, contraband sales, food and clothing exchanges, tobacco sales. I don't have the desire to go there. Furthermore, I think the inmates who attend the yard are viewed differently by the COs and upper staff differently than those of us who choose to work in the unit or remain in a cell or rec rooms.

My cells have always had south exposure. For this I am grateful. It provided me with good natural light in which I draw and write, without the need for harsh artificial lighting.

The vultures, rather the ladies in green I am leaving behind, are becoming more frequent visitors. Since I am leaving, requests have been put in for everything I own, including my non-DOCCS-issued terrycloth shower cap and blanket. Again, I make my kindness gesture clear. The only condition I have is when you leave, you give it to another inmate who can use it. No selling or bartering. It is a pay-it-forward request.

Sleep should never be overrated. Not only is it a good escape from personal woes, it passes the time, and I feel so much stronger for it. Prior to having my children, I would sleep nine to twelve hours a night. Ah, the good old days.

With reference to the library, it is easy to pass info when you know what page to look on. For instance, my sister-in-law was going to send Crest whitening strips in magazines once we agreed on a page number. After some thought, whiter teeth really would not be a great reason to go to lock for 30 days, lol. No, I am not laughing out loud, rather a loss of life, LOL. Locked, no commissary, no packages, and I am unsure about visitation. Why even contemplate the chance? No way. There is a light at the end of this miserable, filthy tunnel.

There's a new protocol. Every day around 4:00 P.M. Count, inmates must present their medical artifacts to the housing CO. Deputy of Security had us take our medical devices out to be photographed. Every day at 4:00 P.M. count I must furnish the CO with the medical devices for verification. My leg compression blowup garment and my knee compression stockings have to be removed from my body for display. Why? What could an old inmate like me do? Do they think I would sneak another individual in or out of the facility in my support hose? They were not interested in my eyeglasses, hearing aids or cane, which I think could double as a weapon. All this nonsense is still stemming from the recent escape of the two violent men from the Clinton CF upstate.

My neighbor returned from Bedford Hills Infirmary. She had to spend the night because the doctor gave her codeine pain medications. No pain medications except for a few NSAIDs and Tylenol are permitted in Taconic. It is nice to see the light on in her room again. My other neighbor is her prison daughter. I took care of her lunch. I gave her my meals on wheels, a meatball sub. I am medically restricted to my cell, so my meals are delivered from the mess hall. When people treat you consistently respectfully, you take good care of them.

This may not be exciting to most, but I am thrilled. Dark clouds are moving in and I can smell the rain in the air. I forgot what rain had smelled like. Oh, no, the ambulance first came and went. An inmate is having an extreme side-effect to her chemo for breast cancer. I am surprised she does not just stay in Bedford Hills infirmary isolation room.

Please move, the "young and immature inmate anywhere else on the compound." Now she is yelling from the kitchen because no one will make her pancakes. Borrow a pan and follow the directions on the box. This girl's name should be "Queen for making everyone miserable." She is always looking for an argument and must have the last word.

I called my ex-husband to see if he was recovered from his stomach bug. He said he was a little better. He thanked me for calling. Weird.

## April 26, 2019, Day 1,359 out of 1,385

I have been awake for a while now. It is pouring rain and I am trying to endure the stabbing pain in my left knee. I am sure it is the rain playing havoc with me again, as this is the knee with the torn interior meniscus. I am not looking forward to walking to medication this morning. The pain is severe enough, though, and I am nauseous from it. I find the more anxious I am to sleep, the more it keeps me awake. Sometimes I am either in too much pain or the restless-leg-syndrome (RLS) is acting up, and I am too anxious to even stay in bed. It is hard to pace in a cell. It is a reminder of the minimal space one needs for survival.

Another inmate needed help with a knitted sock pattern, so after my morning nap I showed her how to pick up the stitches and how to count when the heel is in the right place. There is a Shakespeare play here today. The plays are from a New York City traveling company and they do a good job. I cannot go because of my current medical status.

Why does "The Young Inmate" have to smoke in her room? There is no place here that is smoke free.

I was woken by my hard-of-hearing neighbor. "Mrs. Schonfield, you have to do something. 'Star' is moving into "The Sociopath's" old room." "Star" was on this unit two years ago. Once when she was in the shower, I asked her to turn the volume down on her singing. She responded by stepping out of the shower naked. I walked out after that. Her tirade continued in the hallway in front of my door. On camera, she opened her robe and was threatening a fight. I just stepped into my room. The Sergeant had "Star" put into lockup for 14 days. She cannot come up here, but no other unit is willing to have her.

## April 27, 2019, Day 1,359 out of 1,385. 26 Days and Counting.

I have been counting since day one. I woke up at 3:00, but my body was not hurting like the night before. The slamming sounds of rain against my window stopped before the sun rose over a clear blue sky. There are about four inmates who have stepped up on their notorious personalities, and they clearly have not changed a bit. The sheer volume of their bullying in doorways is enough to make most of us cringe. It is abusive. Very few COs will do anything. I am not afraid of any of them, although with a face recovering from surgery and a knee needing surgery, I am at a disadvantage. Sometimes, I wish we were locked in all day as punishment, but it rarely happens.

Just as I tucked myself in for a morning nap, our CO bellowed, "Schonfield, visit." I went down, hair disheveled and no makeup. It is my sister-in-law. What a welcome and lovely surprise. For four hours, we ate, talked and played Uno. When she left, I picked up the magazines and books she had brought. Unfortunately, the forces I have no control over kept her waiting outside in 40-degree weather for an hour and a half. It is not right how visitors of convicts are treated.

**April 28, 2018, Day 1,360 out of 1,385**

It is cold out and makes for perfect sleep weather. I did not wake between 10:00 P.M. and 6:00 A.M. Counts. I went to make coffee on our shared hot plate with my friend. I am unaware how we got on the topic of guilt and rehabilitation, but she told me why she is here. We cry together. No matter how much progress we make, I believe some pain and guilt will always remain with us.

Another lunch "Meals on Wheels" arrives. Grits, a bagel with cream cheese, sloppy joes, a hamburger roll and re-re-re-cooked vegetables, and it is all at 9:00 A.M. The petite banana looks like it is at the end of the food chain. I am unsure anyone would even consider using this banana as a model for a painting or a drawing. Who would be sadistic enough to put this buffet together and call it brunch?

As I fell asleep from my midday programmed nap, the CO woke me. "Package room." I hoisted myself up, put my shoes on. My hands went through my hair. I grabbed my red commissary-issued bag, came in and trudged down the stairs. My parole clothes are here! My brother sent two bras, eight undies, six pairs of pants, eight shirts, a dress and a jacket, two pairs of shoes, and a leather tote. There was a phone charger in the tote that had to be either sent home at my expense or destroyed immediately. I chose the latter. I was also not allowed the keychain, credit card wallet, watch, or perfume. Alexis will pick it up when she and Eli come in two weeks on Mother's Day.

"Tiny" was moved back from across the street. On occasion, when I had a medical trip over there, I would see her in a solitary area waiting for medical treatment. She looked so disheveled and high. More importantly my neighbor is getting chummy with her.

She is clearly sucked in because she said she knew "Tiny's" history and did not care. I wonder if my neighbor's prison wife will care. Rumor has it that "Tiny" is moving to our housing unit. There are three vacant rooms on our side, the east side. My last three and a half weeks here are going to be a test of my patience. If I pass, there is no reason why I should have to sit through ART, (Aggression Replacement Training), ever.

My brother flew out to visit my dad last night. He checked out the new long-term rehabilitation facility. It is not pretty and shiny, but it is easy to drive to. It has 24-hour security, and the staff insisted on a surprise—an unscheduled visit. Hopefully, my dad will be moving within 30 days. My brother found the deed to our dad's house, so I can get my ex-husband to sign it and get his name off the document. The house looks good, and there is nothing that must be done. All I need now is the interstate transfer, hopefully for the beginning of July.

One of the Spanish women asked me to help her write a remorse letter for her second parole board appearance in June. "The Cartel" is like family to me in here. Of course, I will help. I read the minutes from the final decision from the last board. Since English is not her first language, I have asked her to tell another inmate in Spanish what is in her heart. Then it will be interpreted for me. Tomorrow, we will write the letter.

## April 29, 2019, Day 1,361 out of 1,385

I slept for six hours. Maybe, to sleep at night, all I needed was to be able to breathe. My morning coffee friend gave me a book about her dad to read. In our talk yesterday, she told me the betrayal that landed her in prison. It would seem most often; men have something to do with why women are incarcerated. This is not man-bashing - it's factual.

I wrote to the Nurse Administrator to please move up my hand surgeon appointment. The pain is more persistent, and the swelling evident. My thumb clicks, so I know there is swelling around the nerves and the joint. I saw the nurse on the med line, and she had not received my letter yet. How many days does it take to walk a letter 500 feet?

I remembered to bang on the wall to wake my neighbor this morning. When she sleeps, it is as if she is in a coma. Should one not wake up for count, some COs will issue "disobeying an order" ticket.

It is a quiet morning. Supplies were delivered for May: four bars of soap, six rolls of toilet paper, two bags of sanitary napkins, a toothbrush and toothpaste. This is my last time for supply distribution.

I fell asleep reading the book my coffee friend gave me. It was written about her dad, the police detective who helped take down the Wild Cowboys in New York City—a legendary case in 1995 where one of the most violent drug gangs at that time were convicted. "The convictions represented a major victory for the Homicide Investigation Unit of the Manhattan District Attorney's office, which has concentrated in the last several years on taking down whole drug organizations rather than isolated sellers or individual leaders." I understand why he moved his family to upstate.

I went up to the woman who was our CO today. I thanked her for not being a control freak, always being respectful and fair to me, and I think everyone else. She made me teary when she replied, "I wish all the women were as polite and respectful as you. You do not engage or tolerate the disruptions. You walk away." Thank you, Ma'am.

I was talking with my brother. His appointment with his surgeon was canceled two months ago, but they never called his current phone number, so in disgust, he has made an appointment in July with Dr. John House at the House Institute in California. I think it is pretty funny, "Dr. House," like the TV show. In the middle of the conversation, all the phones went dead, and the cable TV went blank. Once again -- inadequate services were interrupted by the forces in charge.

"Meals-on-Wheels" was vile for lunch: Two hotdog rolls, two pieces of cheese, two pieces of mystery meat, mandarin oranges and soup. I gave the new girl everything except the oranges and the soup. She's our version of "give it to Mikey and see if she likes it." And she does. She stays in her room, except for school. She takes the magazines I have in excess and makes magnificent origami flowers, animals and fruit.

Another parolee came back to our unit. She had left on work release. She had a money crime. She had her license renewed for the business her brother is also a part of. Because of fiduciary responsibilities, it was considered a parole violation—keeping your family employed is irrelevant to DOCCS. Things like this really worry me. I do not want to ever come back to any jail or prison. It is so easy for a P.O. to violate a parolee.

I spent two hours in the clinic waiting to be seen by the nurse. There appears to be a postule in my septum. Finally after literally sitting in her office for two minutes, she put me in to see the doctor tomorrow. I hope it is just irritation and not an infection. My neighbor had stomach pains and she came to the clinic with me.

The new girl from last week who moved up here was confronted tonight for stealing. Of course, she denied it, but the CO made herself clear how theft will not be tolerated in the housing unit.

**April 30, 2019, Day 1,362 out of 1,385**

I have been awake since 4:30 A.M. This is okay because it allowed me to catch up on my letter writing. I am truly blessed to have as many family members and friends who love me and have supported me throughout this incarceration.

After a morning of knitting and napping, I was called to the clinic. The doctor saw the infection in my septum and prescribed Bactrim. At 5:00 P.M., Count was cleared, and I was told by the CO to go to the clinic. No, I do not want to. Fortunately, the doctor allowed the medication nurse to administer my Lyrica early as I didn't know it but I would otherwise have missed my evening dose. I was then stripped and handcuffed, and off to Westchester Medical Center.

Two COs sat with me for three and a half hours in a room to the side of admissions, where we were forgotten. Arthur, a security guard at Westchester Medical Center, made up for it with soup, sandwiches, and a ginger ale. At 9:45, I finally made it into a private room, and out of their massive and crazy busy emergency room. An hour later, my blood was taken. Another CO came and swapped out one of the COs who already worked a double shift. 1:00 A.M., the plastic surgeon came in and took pictures with her phone and sent them to my surgeon. At 3:30 A.M., I was discharged and told to continue the Bactrim and warm moist compresses. The sutures are infected, but IV antibiotics are not necessary.

Due to the hour, I had to go to the Bedford Hills Correctional Facility Regional Medical Unit. We got stuck in their 4:00 A.M. Count, so I was not put upstairs until 5:30 A.M. The Sergeant could have sent me back to Taconic, but instead she just told me to "shut the fuck up," and sent me upstairs. I slept on and off all day until Taconic picked me up and brought me back at 8:30 P.M. It felt so good to peel off the clothes I had worn for more than 24 hours.

## May 2, 2019, Day 1,364 out of 1,385

Maybe DOCCS is really trying to torture me now. Cruella de Vil woke me at 4:30 in the morning for another medical trip. I cannot believe these back-to-back trips. It is very wearing on my body. I hope that I am seeing the hand surgeon for my left thumb. The rain appears miserable and cold. The heat was just put back on in the building. This is the kind of morning when any normal person would just remain in bed, snuggled with blankets. I am not even permitted a hat or a raincoat. I either wear my winter coat or no outerwear.

After today, two Thursdays and I am released. It still does not seem real. I have not tried on my parole clothes yet.

The law library must be furious with me, as every appointment I made, I'm either on a medical trip or at BHCR RMU. I am filing my notice of intent for legal action for my nose, knee and thumb. It is not about money. It is about getting this archaic system to look at the inmates as human beings and not just as a commodity of one-size-fits-all care. Off to the mess hall, where I will sit until 7:00 A.M. and then go for medication and a strip search. I am not going to miss any of this.

Two female officers took me and another inmate to Fishkill Correctional Facility. It is about 45 minutes away. We both saw the hand surgeon. My van mate needs surgery, and I got a needle. A huge needle with lidocaine and some steroids. And when he said, "A pinch," he lied. I believe I shrieked, "Holy Mother of God." All the COs thought it was funny.

Upon return, the CO on the unit unlocked my door and gave me the heads up. "Star" is my new neighbor. LT overrode everyone. It does not matter that she took her clothes off and went to fight me. She leaves in 30 days. I leave in 20. I can do this.

The last time I saw him, Eli asked a very well-thought-out question. "Will I," meaning Eli, "have to sign for Grandma since she's coming home with me?" "No, Eli. No one is responsible for me except me," I told him. I adore this little boy.

The only consistencies are the constant daily inconsistencies at Taconic. Rules constantly change at the discretion of the CO or nurse. I went for my medication only to learn I was not getting my antibiotic. Something happened and no hand-carried medications were delivered tonight. I have a post-surgical infection. I am not missing another dose. The sick-call nurse was busy looking up some girl in her yearbook online. Clearly, I had interrupted her. The physician in the clinic got my chart and found the medication order. The medication clinic has a supply of certain drugs and mine was one of them. I waited 45 minutes, but I got it.

My "coffee" friend came back from carpal tunnel surgery. She went into the infirmary last night as I was leaving. She is in a fair amount of pain. I gave her some crackers for mid-night nausea.

## May 3, 2019, Sunday. Day 1,365 out of 1,385.

It is a weekend, which means we can have visitors. my family is coming to see me. Eli was so funny this morning when he yelled, "20 days, Grandma."

And still no antibiotic. Everyone is commenting on how well I have healed from my rhino recon. I am still a bit swollen, barely bruised. I have no feeling in my upper lip. I am glad I had the surgery. Now I can breathe.

I was called to the draft room and I got to try on the parole clothes. I was so nervous. I know it is silly. I am wearing all blue—including blue sandals—to go home in. Blue, orange, black and gray are forbidden inmate colors. I am giving some of my clothing to other inmates who did not have the luxury of having someone send them parole clothes. I am blessed and I will always share.

No sooner am I awake, someone else gave me another remorse letter to edit. She had gone to Work Release in New York City with Sherry. She said the day after Sherry was not heard from, she overheard the Sergeant tell the CO that "Sherry has probably been trafficked into the sex trade." She just disappeared. No one cared. Too many parolees are turning up missing or dead from overdoses. Why are we a target? And why isn't anything on the news about Sherry? There was barely an investigation. I feel as though parolees are looked at with disgust. We paid our dues.

Society, especially law enforcement, is only concerned when we do something, no matter how trivial, to violate parole and then be returned to prison. I am confident if anyone else not incarcerated were missing, certainly the news would have shown her picture and asked for leads. Just because we have worn green, we are as worthy as someone who has not. Perhaps we are even more virtuous and deserving as we paid our dues. It took a severe punishment and I am leaving stronger, resilient and humbled. I chose the path of doing the work to be a better me, and I am. There is no rehabilitation in NYS DOCCS. I did the work.

I never got to say goodbye to my class or the teacher I spent two years working with. And I was shocked she left an envelope for me. I was so touched that she had the class write in a card wonderful sentiments. Technically the card was contraband by the way it was handed to me by another inmate. I'm greatful for the acknowledgement that I really did make a difference as her IPA, Inmate Prison Assistant, a.k.a. Teacher's Aid. It feels good. I am still medically restricted so no work until my release.

During 4 P.M. Count, someone was humming. The CO unlocked her door and screamed at her saying she was disturbing his Count. Another inmate held her window flap down indicating either using the bathroom or changing clothing. He demanded she get dressed and open her flap immediately. I thought we were allowed the flap down for 15 minutes for that purpose. Rules to safeguard us just do not matter.

I went to the law library and I finally had another inmate help me write my notice of intent to pursue legal action against NYSDOCCS. I am not suing to collect money. I am doing it to get better medical treatment, and I want DOCCS to pay for my knee surgery as it should have been done on their dime since it happened while going on a medical trip.

"The Young Immature One" continued her whiny behavior. She was wearing a former inmate's tight pants and she is about 40 pounds heavier. She was busting out at the seams literally. Finally, we convinced her to change for the "Click-click" photos. Click-click is a Polaroid photo that inmates pay $2 per picture through their commissary, even on visits. It never ceases to amaze me how inmates dress for "Click-click" photos. True, we are in prison. Yet there is more makeup on this compound than in an entire theater troupe. It is sad that even inmates are on a quest to look younger and DOCCs assists. Instead, they should be more concerned with providing nutritious mess hall food or decent medical care. Nope. Makeup wins.

"Star" is part of a unique group of women. This group does not whisper, and they can only scream. Seriously. If you were walking in the direction of the rec room to speak with someone, is it necessary to holler? In trying to recuperate from nose surgery and infection, I placed a sign on my door that read, "Unless you are Governor Cuomo with my signed early release papers, there's a fire, or you happen to be a CO do not wake me." There were chuckles, but quiet ones. I was left alone to sleep.

They are installing forced air vents for A/C. I guess that after having so many ambulances here, at least once a day because of trauma from the heat, it is more feasible to put in the A/C.

## May 4, 2019, Day 1,366 out of 1,385

Technically it is tomorrow, even though it is Tuesday night. I cannot stay asleep. It is 1:17 A.M. and I feel pretty charged up and ready to go. Maybe this is anxiety. I do not want to have to reside with my daughter.

I do not want to fear any slight movement from the directive will land me back here as a parole violator until 2024. I feel like the family dog giveaway. Who wants Fido this weekend?

Everything I helped work for in my marriage is either cut in half or gone. I want to believe I have forgiven the people helped who put me in prison. Perhaps that is just what I tell myself. It is not acceptable to me; I do not own any anger or the pain that accompanies holding a grudge.

Divorce is tough. If you took the marriage at all seriously, divorce feels like a death. And that pain becomes a void. I let myself be the doormat. He stepped all over me, and I let it happen. I loved my husband. I thought somehow, I could do something to prove my love and that he would love me back. I am different now. I am concerned with the dating scene. Perhaps even when things were going south, I felt my relationship with my ex-husband was safe. How do I navigate a new relationship? It will take time for me to adjust.

7:15 A.M. and "Star" and another inmate have the TV on the loudest volume and are laughing louder than a pack of hyenas. I approached the CO and I asked him to address this. He did but it never got quiet. I will not say anything to "Star" that would then lock her in after I asked her to lower her voice. In prison you need to know your audience.

19 days! Alexis informed me that from Taconic we must go straight to Utica for parole. Huge inconvenience. I thought I had 24 hours to appear. I guess not. I can see this post-supervision thing is going to be like working with a demanding travel agent.

I had too much time to ponder today. Perhaps I was just unaware of my impact on others. Just because I was married, two good kids, a community worker, and I had a beautiful home, it in no way dismisses or invalidates the effect of growing up with a mom who was addicted to uppers and alcohol, as well as ignoring the trauma of being raped. My happy ending was not so happy. Ironically, I feel safe and at peace now that I am in prison, around some deranged and feeble-minded maniacs. This is not to say they're are not some inmates of good character as well, as there are plenty.

Today it is the maniacs driving me into silence. Imagine someone turning away every time you go to speak with her. "Young and immature inmate" has borderline personality disorder, amongst other diagnoses, and I am so tired of her endless dramatics. "Midnight" made her stay in the rec room and I was able to say what I wanted to say to her. She claimed I cornered her. I do not know how. She told me I am unnaproachable and not easy to talk to. Instead of staying quiet I said, "Shut the fuck up." This was a far reach from my prison persona.

Another inmate my age and I are going to tag team this and not sound like a bunch of vulgar meth addicts. I hope to never accept being unhappy as normal because it is not. I deserve so much more in the health and happiness departments.

## May 5, 2020: Cinco De Mayo

It is pouring rain, temperatures above 75, and the freaking heat is still on and it feels like the humidity is up to 101 percent.

Surprisingly, I fell asleep with my light on and woke just a few minutes before 6 A.M. Count. Last night, an inmate was clowning around in the rec room and slammed into the bookshelf, eye first. She ran to her room and vomited on the floor, then told our CO she slipped in her room. Otherwise, she could have been issued a ticket and possibly locked for clowning around. Taconic makes no sense. She appears to be okay today.

Well, the unrest in our uncivilized housing unit is escalating. "My Coffee Friend" was trying to sleep while two inmates were in the hallways making a ridiculous amount of noise. "My Coffee Buddy" said something, so the inmates made even more noise just to piss her off. The drama escalated. Someone else got involved. Next ,"Midnight" got involved too and tried to provoke one of the women to hit her. Trying to sleep here is unheard of. Far from being a unit everyone used to hope to live on, this place has turned into something worse than horrible. 18 days left. I just have 18 more days. All of this just when I thought things could not get any worse.

The mix of inmates housed on my unit is getting very volatile and dangerous. One troublemaker tried provoking my friend on for a fight after "my coffee buddy" got mad and asked "Star" to be respectful of other people. "Don't tell me what to do." "Let's take it to the showers." "Come on and try. Use your hands on me...." This is what I listen to in my earbuds, even with music on. It is beyond rude, obnoxious and immature. These women are very rough. 17 days and a wake-up to go. Point of reference: There are no cameras in the showers.

## May 6, 2019, Day 1,368 out of 1,385

It is 1:15 A.M. I was startled from a sound sleep by our CO yelling, "Whoever's smoking, this is your warning before I write a ticket." I am so disgusted with this "everybody pays" attitude. I have sleep issues on my best days. It was not necessary to wake me. On the other hand, I wonder if our resident smokers are the reason I wake up at random times. Ramadan is here and two of my neighbors will be participating and will be unlocked at 3:00 A.M. to shower and go to the mosque. Last year, it felt like I was sharing their holiday, as I was woken from the water hitting the tiles in the shower.

Now they have implemented a phone list for 7:00 A.M. to 3:45 P.M. as well. The arguing continues. Soon there will be a list for flushing one's toilet, almost asleep, when the CO came and told me I had to go to the clinic. The doctor saw me and was actually pleased and not dismissive. The infection in my nasal sutures is a good old staph infection, thankfully not MRSA.

I am using up my yarn and making a scrap scarf. It is easy, and it keeps me focused.

I am well versed in keeping enemies close. One must know their strengths and weaknesses. With "Star" living up here, I made peace. The floors are being stripped and waxed. Of course, it is inmates doing the work. She needed very hot water for the floor stripping chemicals, so I volunteered with my hotpot. She and I started talking. When she is not being an aggressive person, she is okay to be around.

## May 7, 2019, Day 1,369 out of 1,385

16 days to go. First, those celebrating Ramadan were woken at 3:00 A.M., along with two inmates right across from me. As I dozed off, the CO unlocked my door. "Medical trip." Rhino recon follow-up. I was in the mess hall by 5:30 A.M. "Princess" was there. She is being released but deported to Haiti. She must go to Albion Correctional Facility, and then on the 10th of May, she will fly out. She was our kitchen connection whenever we needed certain foods for holiday celebrations. My trip to Westchester Medical Center was easy. I had two very chilled COs. The head of recon surgery looked at my nose. Everyone agreed not to add on extra days of the antibiotics. No one in the room was pleased having to speak with Dr. C. at Taconic. It was futile. I am not sure she's a licensed physician

It is a noisy day. Maintenance is replacing pipes everywhere. Air conditioning vents are being installed. Actually, it is not a/c vents; they are putting air circulation vents into the cells. Let us circulate poor quality, hot air. Am I the only one concerned about the asbestos dust? The workers have on masks and goggles. The inmates, of course, do not.

I have no anger left in me right now. In the end of this bid. Maybe my rage was directed once at my ex-husband. There is no ceiling that I cannot break through. I know my strengths and my weaknesses. I think I have a clear understanding of myself, and it feels good. I feel empowered.

## May 8, 2019, Day 1,370 out of 1,385

Eli told me I have 14 days and a wake-up.

I am getting the "short and shitty," almost out the gate prison attitude. The "young inmate" just walking the halls irritated me. When she starts whining, I just must walk away before I say something beneath my character. The heat is still on. These people make no sense. It is 70 degrees outside. Another older inmate asked me to buy her black beans on my last commissary run tomorrow. I knew this was coming, because she gave me a box of unsolicited crackers earlier in the week. No good deed goes without payback.

I was walking with the CO on my way to medications this morning. She was in the operating room with me when I had the rhino reconstruction. I know why I hurt now. My nose was just cut and peeled back toward my forehead. She said it looked like the head of a skeleton.

For the love of God! "The young inmate" is getting high sniffing in the yard. Does that girl even want to get out of prison?

The Sergeant came up to the unit and instead of saying, "Ladies, things are looking better, but I don't want you hanging clothing day-to-day on your radiators or headboards," she barked, "There will be no bras and panties hanging on your bed or on the radiator." She walked away. Clearly, she has never read up on how to make friends and gain cooperation.

## May 9, 2019

A 26-year-old inmate from Bedford Hills Correctional Facility hanged herself. "My coffee Friend" found out yesterday on her medical trip. What is even sadder is she was due for release in August. Even if it was not a suicide, DOCCS will cover it up.

Alexis' landlord is not thrilled I will be residing with her for a few months. I suppose if I had not had this experience, I would not want someone on parole living in my rental either. It is remarkable how perspectives change, and the paradigm shifts after breaking the law and being a guest of the NYSDOCCS.

My nose is looking good. I believe the infection is gone. I may have to go to the clinic today. It has been three days of excruciating left ear pain, and I had hoped it was swelling moving around. Let us see what the morning may bring.

It is 5:30 A.M., and the mess hall workers were just called. I put my door flap down to use the bathroom when a moment later, there is a knocking on my door. I thought I was allowed 15 minutes. When a CO, or anyone for that matter, knocks on your door when the flap is down, the inmate must respond with a reason as to what they are doing. Once

I thought I was being funny, and said, "I'm constipated, and you're interrupting my process." It did not go over so well.

A Spanish woman was taken to lock yesterday. I do not know the details, but apparently, through inmate gossip channels, we heard she was masturbating in her cell and the Sergeant caught her. This goes back to several previous thoughts. If this place is rehabilitative, it cannot be effective by eliminating basic human needs, so I will go with the concepts of rehabilitation for incarceraded individuals who contnue to be oppressed. What exactly is being corrected? Masturbation can be done quietly and discreetly. It relieves stress, and there is an exorbitant amount of stress on this compound. We are not allowed to touch each other at all. No hugs or any gesture of comfort for that matter. A hug can get you in lock. I was told in graduate school a healthy human being needs at least eight hugs a day. How is a person supposed to reenter society when they have been denied basic human touch? My point is, why did she go to lockup for something nothing more than self-soothing and ingrained in the animal kingdom? In the same sense, I fail to see the demands for a drug-free prison system. Assuming an inmate is incarcerated for abusing illicit substances, how does it make sense to punish them more severely after the judge has already sentenced them for feeding their addiction? After this incarceration detour, I can understand why someone would want to be high. I have never been interested in that type of self- medication, though I had thought about the benefits of a drug-induced coma until my release date.

This is a new request. Two inmates came up and asked me to draw up a marriage license for them. Do I look like a lawyer? They are each other's wives, and one of them is being released the same day I am. For some reason, I feel like Mrs. Google. If you need information or have a question, just show up at my door. Sometimes, I believe there really is a neon sign above my door that reads, "24-Hour Bodega and Information Room."

I have learned in prison how to have a disagreement and let it go and not dwell. Angry one day, the next day you may look out for each other. "Star" is such a case. We look out for each other in trying to get a phone slot. I have also realized how judgmental I used to be. I would prefer just exercising good judgment. I've always told my kids, "Why is subjective. It does not matter. How and what are the better questions." I did not fail in my so-called life. While this is a path I would not have sought, it has been a time of healing for me and learning things inside that I never could have and never would have believed before.

## May 11, 2019, 12 Days, or 11 Days and a Wake-up

I seem to rise with the birds.

We have had a really, pleasant overnight CO. He does not make us stand. We just wiggle a foot and show that we are alive. Then he shuts the lights. "Coffee" and I were in the kitchen, making our morning brew at 6:30 in the morning. No one was up moving until 7:20. It was lovely.

I began to write my letters to the women I am leaving behind. It is not as easy as I had thought. Everyone except "my coffee friend" and me are sleeping. "The young one" wakes up and starts pacing the halls on the hunt for everything necessary to make pancakes. As she passes each and every room demanding pancake mix, a bowl, a spoon, inmates are screeching back for her to just shut up. She stops in the hallway and starts yelling, "Don't tell me what to do." 11 days, and I just need to remain in my chill zone for 11 days.

It would seem, that all drama here involves "the young one." It is absolutely maddening. She did not sign up to use the kitchen, yet she feels entitled to use the kitchen during my slot to make pancakes. Really, two hours? She started yelling, then shrieking, and "Coffee" said she was going to throw "the young one's" frying pan onto the floor. Then "the young one" repeated over and over, how she was going to punch "my coffee friend" in the face. Fortunately, we have a decent CO, and she put an end to it without calling the Sergeant. There was an outdoor rec at 1:00 P.M., and thankfully, "the young one" went out. She is young, very immature and very manic. I am just staying in my room with my doors closed. The behavior exhibited by many of these women makes me feel like I either lived under a rock for most of my life or I am just extremely naïve. Both may be true.

I have been playing "This Is Your Life, Melisa Schonfield" in my head. I have nothing, and yet I have so much. I am scared, of starting over. What if I am very, successful? What if I am not? I suppose, regardless of the direction I choose, the feelings are the same: anxiety, fear of success, fear of being unsuccessful. I am choosing success, and when I am willing to do the work to get there, I need guidance.

## May 12, 2019, Mother's Day, Day 1,374 out of 1,385

It is my fourth and last Mother's Day in the big house. It is miserable outside. Alexis and Eli are coming, and I hope they are wearing raincoats with hoods. I have four boxes of stuff I am sending them back with. My room is empty. It looks like I am a newbie instead of an old-timer. I have expunged my life, giving so much away.

"My Coffee Friend" and I enjoyed the quiet until 7:30. It was delightfully calm. I waited and waited for Alexis and Eli to appear on the walkway. At 10:55 A.M., they came running in the pouring rain. I raced down to the visiting room, just making 11:00 A.M. count. There is a professional makeup artist and a photographer for the inmates today, at no cost to any of us. It was very nice. We received one photo each. I can see how prison has aged me. Wow. Eli became teary-eyed when it was time for him to leave. I cheered him up with, "Ten days and a wake-up. This is your last visit here. I'm coming home." He smiled and hugged me. Holy shit, 10 days and a wake-up. It is not real. None of this has seemed real. I keep hoping DOCCS was a nightmare I would wake up from only to be surrounded by my family and friends. Clearly, it has been real.

I spoke with my ex-husband today. He was concerned that I had not called him in two weeks. What he fails to realize is how I have moved on with a life that no longer includes him. He could not answer why he stopped visiting me two and a half years ago. I am not resuming my old life again. It no longer exists. I am no longer the dentist's wife. I no longer live in my forever home. I have no car. Much of what I have collected over 40 years ago is gone. Yet I am not hurt and sad, or even angry. I have lived with such minimal things over the last four years that it really does not matter. I am sure I will still enjoy designer labels, et cetera, but I no longer must fend off my feelings of despair with shopping trips for nothing specifically in mind. I think I made shopping a recreational activity.

I have been forced to use a toenail clipper not only for trimming nails, but as a paper cutter, knitting scissors and even cutting my pants for hemming. Oops, we are not supposed to cut them, as it is altering or destroying state property.

I do not know what it is going to feel like to leave on the 23rd. I will not have on any mascara, as I anticipate overwhelming feelings of joy to be finished with the severest part of my punishment. But I am apprehensive living with all the rigid rules of post- supervision. With so many women I have met through the years returning here on parole violations, I think my fears are justified. I cannot wait to begin my fight for prison reform, and in the same breath, I fear the haters and the unyielding politics, as well as the obstinate thinkers, as I pursue this change.

I am sure there will always be someone eager to remind me how I committed a heinous crime and did hard time. For them, I hope to deliver a standard response: I was sentenced by a judge and served my time, and I would like to look forward not backwards. I do not want to waste energy on the people who will have opinions of me before even hearing me introduce myself. I took the years of punishment for this crime.

Eli asked what I want to eat when I am released. I do not care. It will not be food allocated in a monthly package, nor will it be soy-filled mess hall food. I need a complete physical, and to get healthy again, and take it from there. I cannot wait to take a shower without shower shoes, and I will not need to change in my room into a robe and drag all of my toiletries down to a shower room. I long to see a bathtub filled with hot water and bubbles. I want to put on my music, dim the lights and soak until my skin looks like prunes and the water turns cold. I want to use sunscreen on my face, hair color and shampoo, and creams with alcohol in them. I cannot wait to see my face in 15X magnification, a real glass-lit mirror.

Then there is my electric toothbrush. I can wear patterned and underwire bras and spandex. I can wear lace lingerie. I want to rest my head on a fluffy pillow and a comfortable bed. I think I might have an affair with my washing machine, or my fridge and freezer. Oh, how I long to have real metal scissors again. I hope not to have any keys. I prefer keyless entry and a keypad retinal display. I do not want to hear keys jingling. It will be interesting who calls me first. No one has been able to phone me since August 19, 2015. I had to call them, and only if their name was approved and the party was to put money on the telephone account.

As obnoxious as many of these stereotypical inmates have been, I will miss them. In the truest sense of the word we have become family. Ironically though when I leave, I cannot associate with anyone in prison or parole, but I will never forget them. To forget means history can repeat itself. I have evolved into a humbled, peaceful and complete woman. My intelligence and sense of humor are intact. Make no mistake, my kindness is not a coverup for weakness. I am kind because, in my heart, I will always be a social worker. I have learned to say no and walk away and not to do just anything for love. If you do not stand up for something, then you stand for nothing.

The Rabbi said goodbye to me last week. She paid me a huge compliment, telling me how I transformed myself and stood up for my beliefs without having to offend anyone else. The Rabbi is a delightful woman. She is an intelligent feminist before her time.

There was another rabbi who counseled me earlier, whose words I will never forget:

September 2, 2016 29 Av, 5776
Melisa Schonfield 15G0717
Taconic CF 250 Harris Rd
Bedford Hills NY 10507-2497

Dear Melisa,

It is important to look at things from both ends. What kind of man were you married to, that the moment you are experiencing some problems, he deserts you! You have given him your life and more and now that you have some problems, he does not consider them his as any normal man would, but runs away? It means you never had him to begin with and maybe this is for the better.

Love stands above being a felon or age, when the right man will come into your life, I assure you that he is not going to measure you up in that you have a felony on your record. Of course, when meting someone, you do not tell that person at the first meeting that you were once in prison, but I believe that the prison experience can make you more sensitive. The key is in your hands, because being bitter will pull you down.

I am enclosing a Book on the experience of the Holocaust, Dare to Survive, to allow you to see a period in life where things looked extremely bleak and yet she made it. Your situation is nothing compared to what the book describes, and I assure you that you too will survive.

Imagine a brilliant teacher, a professor of world-renowned profundity, whose writings require advanced degrees to comprehend. This teacher is working in his office, analyzing, thinking, delving into the deepest thoughts.

Just outside his door at the university is the janitor, mopping the hallway. The janitor is a simple man, without a "higher" education. He would not understand the basics of the professor's field; an advanced degree for him is not even a question. For him to have any inkling of what the professor is studying is utterly inconceivable.

Obviously, the professor and the janitor have no connection. The thoughts of one operate in a different dimension than the thoughts of the other. But then the professor, hearing the janitor outside his door, asks if the janitor would please bring him a drink of water. And at that moment, a connection is begun, the lines of communication are open and a relationship becomes possible.

The teacher does not necessarily need the water. He is not particularly thirsty. He just wants a drink. Such a request comes not from logic but an exertion of his will. It's a desire, and a desire, the inner urge of the soul, defies reason.

Now if the janitor brings the professor a glass of water, the connection is made and the relationship established. Connect with the Infinite G-d, only the difference between us and Him is vastly, immeasurably, infinitely greater than the distance between the professor and the janitor.

G-d asks us to perform mitzvot (commandments). And when we do, when we fulfill His will, not because it makes sense, not because there's a reason, not even because we accomplish something, but simply because He asks, because He wants us to do that action, then, and only then, do we establish a relationship.

Indeed, the word "mitzva" means not just "commandment," but "connection." When we respond to the command, we connect.

But there's one last point: Let's go back to our analogy.

Our tradition uses analogies to help us understand how we can have a connection with the Infinite Source of our being. If the teacher asks for a glass of water, but is brought soda, beer, or even orange juice, not to mention ice cream or cake (what if he has a sugar problem?), his request is not being fulfilled. The connection isn't there. Because the only way to make that connection is to fulfill the request, to do what is asked, not what the janitor thinks.

And the same is true with mitzvot. There's a right way to do them the way that will fulfill G-d's request, detailed for us in the Code of Jewish Law. And that's how we connect with G-d.

I am grateful to her.

**May 23, Day 1385**

I am being released today. According to the DOCCS website:

"Taconic Correctional Facility, is located in Bedford Hills New York, part of Westchester County. It is a medium security prison that houses females. While incarcerated at Taconic Correctional Facility inmates can earn an adult basic education and GED. Additionally, inmates can take college courses and earn credits through programs offered by several local colleges. Taconic Correctional Facility offers inmates vocational training in cosmetology, business, painting, and decorating. Alcoholics Anonymous meetings are also available to inmates, as well as substance abuse treatment services and a Female Trauma Recovery program. These programs are not always available.

"Mission Statement: To improve public safety by providing a continuity of appropriate treatment services in safe and secure facilities where all inmates' needs are addressed and they are prepared for release, followed by supportive services for all parolees under community supervision to facilitate a successful completion of their sentence.

"**Goals:**

- Create and maintain an atmosphere where all inmates, parolees, staff, volunteers and visitors feel secure.

- Develop and implement individualized treatment plans for each inmate and parolee that includes post release reentry plans.

- Teach inmates and parolees the need for discipline and respect, and the importance of developing a principled work ethic.

- Establish a risks/needs/responsivity approach to programming, treatment, and community supervision to ensure a continuity of services.

- Assist all staff by providing the requisite training and resources needed to perform their duties while enhancing their skills.

- Offer career development opportunities for all staff.
- Ensure workforce stability through mentoring and succession planning.

**"Values**

- Operate with ethical behavior.
- Recognize the value of each person.
- Protect human dignity.
- Offer leadership and support to all.
- Offer respect and structure at all times."

None of this is true.

It is a disservice to the individual, family, and society as a whole to only look at the choices those in power deem illegal. In order to carry out true rehabilitation it is essential to look at all the events that lead up to the crime.

I cannot pretend the experience has not damaged me or those who love me. It has left us all feeling infuriated at the lack of checks and balances and, in the end, it left us all feeling helpless. The judicial system needs to catch up with the psychological community. It is absurd to deceive society with mandated sentencing when every arrest brings different circumstances to lead a person to that tipping point. It is not simply about breaking the law—it's about what happened to get you to break the law because you deeply believed there was no other choice.

I have not been "rehabilitated." But I have had time to think and learn and meditate. I will leave here today free from the prison of a marriage with a man I mistakenly trusted with my life. I have paid the ultimate price not just with time served, but with time lost, relationships gone, being invisible. There is no justice for me on the other side. My ex-husband walks freely. POSSD who abused and bullied my daughter and grandson roams freely. Another man who abused and bullied and raped me, forcing me to get an illegal abortion when I was a teenager, still plays freely. They have all been free all along. Now I, too, am free, in every sense of the word.

Today I pack up, throw out my past? It cannot be thrown away. I won't be thrown away either. I did my time and paid my debt to society. I made a huge mistake and the punishment was quite severe. Perhaps I lost my mind. I am angry that the systems put in place to intervene, assist, and rehabilitate somehow circumvented my family and me. Who knows how things might have turned out if the police had handled POSSD, if social services had played a role, if I hadn't taken the fall alone, if the judicial system represented me more effectively, and if DOCCS was geared toward restoration and/or rehabilitation in any way at all. But I will not look back. I do not even want to glance in the proverbial rearview mirror. How could that help me now in any way? It would only make me bitter, and I will never be bitter. I am much better than that now.

Officer: Please unlock my door. I am ready.

# POSTSCRIPT

Statistics on Women in Prison in the United States:
- 6.8 percent of the nation's inmates are female.
- Drug offenses make up roughly 46 percent of all sentences.
- Homicide and related offenses make up 3.2 percent of all sentences.
- Immigration offenses make up 7.5 percent of all sentences.

The US has more correctional facilities than any other country on Earth.

Across the country, women in prison are disciplined at higher rates than men—often two to three times more often—for smaller infractions of prison rules. That was one finding of an investigation by NPR and the Medill School of Journalism at Northwestern University in 2018.

The ACLU reports that there are currently 219,000 women—mostly mothers—behind bars in our nation's overlapping criminal justice systems. Only five percent of the world's female population lives in the U.S., yet nearly one-third of the world's female prisoners are here in the United States.

As recently as 1997, 12 states had no laws prohibiting sexual contact between women and their jailors: Alabama, Kentucky, Massachusetts, Minnesota, Montana, Nebraska, Oregon, Utah, Vermont, Washington, West Virginia and Wisconsin.

How is incarceration supposed to help anyone at all? Causation. Feedback Loops. Chaos Theory. All systems are subject to this pattern. It is not useful to understand human behavior through searching for linear, one-directional cause-effect relationships. It serves little purpose to ask "why" persons do what they do. A more useful inquiry is "how" or in what way something happened. "A interacts with B to produce AB, which changes both A and B, and results in C, which is partly A, B, and AB." I am C. I will forever be C, a product of the systems that failed to take care of me.

There was a paper written in 1934 called WHY PRISONS FAIL by Ray Mrs. Simpson. It was prescient:

> It is common knowledge that penal institutions are failing to provide suitable programs of character development inside their vine-clad walls. Officials in charge of these institutions should not be severely blamed for this state of affairs because most of them are well aware of these facts but do not know what to do about it. One cannot place too much blame upon politics either. The outstanding feature of the whole situation seems to be the evident fact that specific techniques and methods for changing or developing desirable human conduct are wretchedly inadequate. This lack of method is felt not only by prison administrators but by teachers and parents as well. There is urgent need for some definite program of research to determine how to develop traits of honesty, trustworthiness and play which might be turned into practical use in reorganizing the programs of penal institutions.

In order to get better in there, you have to really work to change everything. I did the work.

Staying bitter or seeking better is a choice. I made the choice to deal with the bitterness head on, and though I will remember everything, I am a better person. I realized who I am never changed. I finally gave myself permission to be me. I did the work and continue everyday to make sure I live a better not bitter life. I don't recommend what I did to others and would not suggest anyone to go through what I have experienced (rape, prison, etc).

I have been released. When I went through the gate Eli hugged me. He was holding balloons in one hand and a dozen red roses in the other. Suddenly he began to cry and he sobbed, "Grandma, please never leave me again." I will not. He said, "Grandma, please never leave me again." I will not.

DOCCS forgot to release my medications along with me. No doctor will prescribe them without an examination, and no doctor is available to examine me for several weeks. Withdrawal could also be the new norm of my life. When I went to prison the normal I had became a distant memory of what normal is now that I am a parolee. Withdrawal symptoms, from my prescriptions, include headache, mood changes, nausea, insomnia, diarrhea, seizures and suicidal ideation. Out of prison yet sentenced to misery—yet another example of systems that simply do not function. They don't give you the medications you need when you are prisoner; they don't give you the medications you need when you are free, and in between, they don't do anything to rehabilitate you. Every step of the way, they set you up to fail.

I was robbed of everything when I went to prison. I was robbed of so much when I was released from prison. I miss my prison family. I miss them showing up by cell door and asking me for help with schoolwork or knitting. I miss the prison sorority. These women I lived with protected me, in spite of how different we were; they had my back as much as I had theirs. We supported each other like family.

Now I'm not allowed to have any contact with them until I am off of parole (This has since been reformed and as long as all parties are law-abiding, socialization is permitted) Can you imagine? The system cut me off from the support system I created in order to survive. I have been robbed of my community, banned from the people who went through this with me, all together. It makes no sense. Soldiers are encouraged to be with other soldiers, veterans with veterans who have experienced the trenches. But ex-felons are sentenced to be alone.

I am lucky to have a family on the outside. Eli and I have baked cookies. I am living with him and Alexis. It is imperfect, but it is home for now. I took myself to our local diner, and nobody recognized me. It was fantastic. I have had real eggs, and rye toast with butter, and a veggie burger. I thought my first meal after release would be sushi. Funny how I forgot about wanting that at all.

But life is not the same. I am not the same. I know I feel incredibly nervous by the way people look back at me, curious and uncomfortable. At least I have stopped having that recurring dream about my old life. I am glad that is gone.

I put an offer on a house. It will be mine and mine alone, mine without a husband. I did not need a man to make this happen. I am self-sufficient in ways I never knew I could be. This is my fresh start. My new self. And with that, I will move forward, not as a victim, not as a prisoner, but as my better self with the best of my life yet to come.

...And she lived happily ever after